一城泉水

中共济南市委宣传部

山东城市出版传媒集团·济南出版社

Jinan:

A City
Enriched by
Famous Springs

前言

济南，古称泺邑、历下邑，汉高后元年（前187）始称济南，至今已有2200多年的历史。古城济南，山灵水秀，文脉绵长。"四面荷花三面柳，一城山色半城湖""海右此亭古，济南名士多"……这些名句是对济南城市风貌和人文历史的真实写照。

济南，又称"泉城""泉都"。得益于济南地区独特的地质结构和地理环境，形成了四大泉域、十大泉群、七十二名泉，总计800多处天然涌泉，使这里成为名冠天下的天然岩溶泉水博物馆。

古城济南，因泉而兴。"家家泉水，户户垂杨"，生活在这里的人们世代与泉为伴，依泉而居。不竭的泉水，也滋养和造就了济南历史上一代代文人：李清照、辛弃疾、张养浩、边贡、李攀龙、王士禛……

多姿多彩的泉水，是古城兴盛和发展的基因与血脉，也是济南亘古不变的城市名片。向世人展示、推介济南泉水风采和泉水文化，是每一个生于斯、长于斯的泉城人的责任担当。济南摄影家李华文先生，以镜头为画笔，以光影为油彩，以名泉为画布，多年坚持不懈，探迹寻踪，遍访名泉。他的作品通过细节的再现、光影的刻画、视角的锤炼，展现了济南泉水的轻灵明秀、宁静自然之美。

用泉水文化传承济南历史文化内涵，体现当代生活品质，弘扬省会城市精神，彰显泉城时代风采，是我们策划这部作品的初衷。细细品味济南、品味泉水，可以感受这方热土的过去与未来、妩媚与粗犷、机智与敦厚、礼仪与豁达、富足与幸福、平凡与辉煌！

《一城泉水》编委会
2019年5月

Foreword

In ancient times, Jinan was first called "Luoyi" and "Lixiayi", and it was called "Jinan" since 187 B.C. So it has a history of more than 2200 years. As an old city, Jinan is famous for its beautiful natural sceneries and cultural heritage. "Daming lake is decorated by lotuses and surrounded by willows, and half of the city's the mountain scenery is reflected on the surface of the lake." "This pavilion in Shandong has a long history, and the city of Jinan has a long list of celebrities." These famous lines are a faithful reflection of the landscapes and civilization of Jinan.

Jinan is now also called "the city of springs" and "the Big City of Springs". Thanks to its unique geologic structure and geographical environment, Jinan has 4 spring areas, 10 spring groups and the 72 famous springs out of more than 800 springs. It is a world-famous museum of natural springs.

The old Jinan city was prosperous for its springs. "Every family has spring water, whose willows are everywhere." People in Jinan have lived in accompany with springs for generations. The inexhaustible spring water nourishes a long list of scholars in Jinan, e.g., Li Qingzhao, Xin Qiji, Zhang Yanghao, Bian Gong, Li Panlong, Wang Shizhen…

The colorful spring water is the gene and bloodline of Jinan's prosperity and development, which is also the eternal name card of Jinan. It is our obligation to show the charm and culture of Jinan's springs to the world. Mr. Li Huawen, who was born in Jinan, consistently visits and takes photos of the famous springs, as if an artist paints pictures with colorful natural oils. The representation of details, depiction of light and shadow, and selection of camera angles in Mr. Li's compositions faithfully show the lightness, brightness and serenity of the springs in Jinan.

This album is designed with the original intention to inherit the historical and cultural connotation of Jinan, represent the quality and charm of modern life, and carry forward capital city spirits. A fine taste of Jinan and its springs will help you to perceive the city's history and future, loveliness and boldness, wisdom and honesty, politeness and open-mindedness, affluence and happiness, commonness and glory.

Editorial Board of
Jinan: A City Enriched by Famous Springs
2019.5

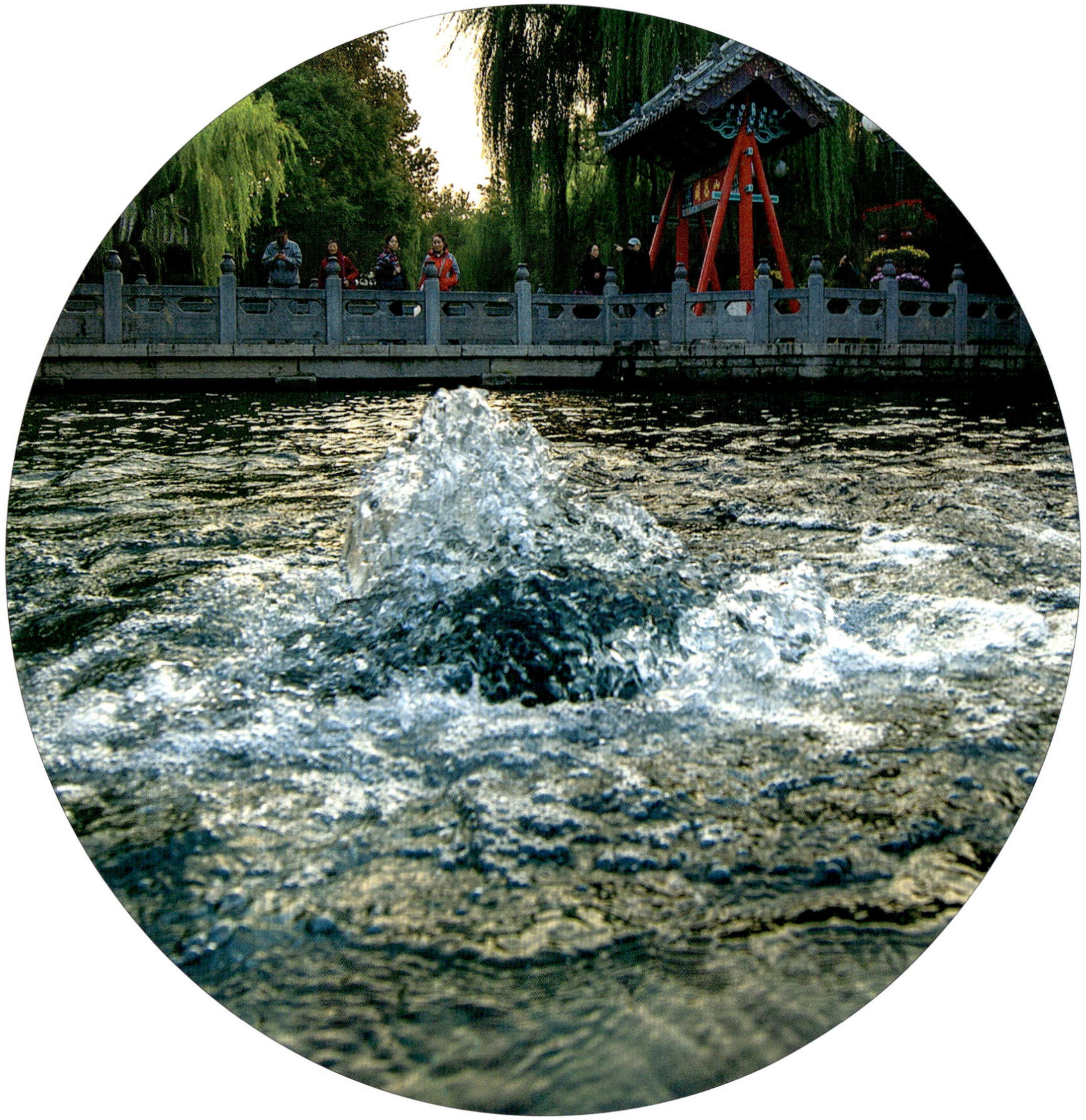

汩汩泉水里冒出的城

济南，是一座泉的城市。

济南，是从汩汩泉水里冒出来的。

"家家泉水，户户垂杨"，这是刘鹗在《老残游记》中对济南的生动描绘。

济南泉多，多到至今也没人能够数清。所以有诗人说，借问济南多少泉，请数一数济南人的眼睛。济南泉水资格老，随便指出一个泉来，岁数都会让人惊讶得合不拢嘴，最早见诸文字记载的趵突泉就已有3500年历史。济南泉水奇特，那气魄，那气派，那气度，连皇帝都叹为观止。"天下奇观""天下泉城""天下泉都"的美誉实实在在，并不虚泛。

"趵突腾空"作为济南的奇妙景观之一，具有可观、可闻、可品、可触的文化特点。眼可观其水势，《水经注》形容该泉"泉源上奋，水涌若轮"；耳可闻其水声，赵孟𫖯诗曰"波涛声震大明湖"；口可品其水味，乾隆皇帝南巡"一路饮玉泉水，至此换趵突泉水"；手可触其水冷，王钟霖《第一泉记》称："趵突甘而淳，清而冽，且重而有力，故潜行远，而鼍腾高。"趵突泉，诚可谓"一景四奇"。

珍珠泉因平地涌泉、腾如珠串而得名。它位于济南古城中心，早在1600多年前的北魏时期，便为许多文人学士所青睐。人们经常聚于溪畔池岸作"曲水流觞"之饮，并将泉池誉称为"流杯池"。清代散文大家王昶在他的《游珍珠泉记》中这样描绘当时的泉景："泉从沙际出，忽聚忽散，忽断忽续，忽急忽缓，日映之，大者为珠，小者为玑，皆自底以达于面，瑟瑟然，累累然。"

王府池子原来是王爷的园池，如今隐藏在曲曲折折的老街旧巷里，属于民间了。今日走在池畔的胡同里，青石板铺就的街道、潺潺的流水、简约的石板桥、古色古香的对联，还有那一不小心跳出来的泉眼，不禁让你怀疑自己来到了江南。王府池子是一幅悠然的画，小桥、流水、人家，清净温婉的氛围里，飘散着泉文化的浓厚韵味。

还有黑虎泉，黑虎咆哮，喷玉吐雪，琵琶泉，泉声"嘈嘈切切错杂弹，大珠小珠落玉盘"；九女泉，听这名字，就知道那泉眼里冒出来的，肯定是一个魅力神话。

济南的泉，纯净，清澈，如同济南人的心境；济南的泉，又不安静，如沸如涌，就像济南人的热情。游赏济南泉景，解说是多余的，情感是要溢出来的。济南到处都是汩汩泉眼，来一次你是看不够的。你贪婪地看过她们后，静静地闭上眼睛，就会沉醉。坐在一眼眼泉畔小憩，你会觉得她很奇妙，很令人心颤，她的美丽充满张力。泉面上弥漫着摄人心魄的氤氲，融汇着济南文化的安详。倾听，你就能听见这个城市生命的律动和勃发前的沉静。

济南，满城泉水。济南，满街泉香。济南，满地泉韵。这座从泉水里冒出来的城市有着百样华姿、千般奇景。清澈甘美的泉水滋润了济南，给这座城市带来了数不尽的风情和说不尽的意蕴。

到这样一座城市来慢慢品泉，肯定是一件赏心悦目的事。

那么，就跟着我们心灵的镜头，去看看那一汪汪灵动的清泉吧。

The City
that Emerges
from Springs

Jinan is a city of springs.

Jinan emerges from the spring water.

"Every family has spring water, whose willows are everywhere." This is Liu E's portrayal of Jinan in *The Travels of Lao Can*.

There are many springs in Jinan, and so far no one can tell the exact number of them. Therefore, a poet said that if you ask how many springs there are in Jinan, please count the eyes of the people of Jinan. Jinan springs boast a long history, and the age of each spring is astonishing. According to the latest archaeological findings, Baotu Spring, which was first seen in written records, has a history of 3,500 years. These are countless beautiful words to praise the distinctiveness of the impressive springs in Jinan. Even the emperors of different dynasties marveled at them. The reputations of "The Wonders of the World", "The Springs City under the Heaven" and "The Big City of Springs under the Heaven" indeed come naturally from real distinction.

As one of the wonderful landscapes of Jinan, "Baotu Rising High into the Air" has its cultural characteristics in terms of sense of sight, sense of smell, sense of taste and sense of touch. Its potential can be seen. In *Commentary on the Waterways Classic*, it was thus described: "the water sprays high and runs like rolling wheels". Its voices can be heard. The poet Zhao Mengfu said, "The sound of waves shakes the Daming Lake." Its flavor can be tasted. When Emperor Qianlong visited Jinan, he said, "I drink water from the Yuquan all along the way, and when I come here I start to drink Baotu Spring Water." Its coldness can be touched. In his *Record of the First Spring*, The officer of the Qing Dynasty Wang Zhonglin said, "Baotu is sweet, clear and strong, heavy and powerful, because the source of the water is deep underground, so it sprays very high. The Baotu Spring can be faithfully described as a scene of four "wonders".

Zhenzhu Spring, also called Pearl Spring, which got its name because it gushed out from flat ground and looked like a string of pearls in the sky. It is located in the center of the ancient city of Jinan. As early as 1600 years ago in the Northern Wei Dynasty, the area was favored by many literary scholars, who often gathered at the banks to drink. This pool is known by them as "Pool with Flowing Glasses". In the Qing Dynasty, prose writer Wang Chang described the spring scene in his *Record of Traveling to Pearl Spring*: "The spring flows from the sand. It suddenly gathers and suddenly disperses. It suddenly becomes hurry and suddenly slows down. It suddenly disappears and suddenly continues. The sun shines on the spring water. The big ones are round beads, and the little ones are non-round beads, and they all reach the surface from the bottom."

Wangfu Pond originally belonged to a royal family. It is now hidden in the old lanes of the winding old streets, which belongs to the common people. Nowadays, in the alleyways next to the pool, you can see the streets paved with blue stones, the flowing water, simple stone bridges, antique couplets, and accidentally sighted springs, which make you really wonder whether you are in the south of the Yangtze River. Wangfu Pond is like a leisure painting with bridges, running water and families. The clean and gentle atmosphere permeates the charm of spring culture.

Heihu Spring is roaring, and the spouting spring is like jade and snow. The sound of Pipa Spring looks as if the verse: "loud and soft sounds are mixed, just like big and tiny pearls falling on a jade plate." As for Jiunyu Spring, also called Nine Fairy Maidens Spring, when you hear this name, you know that what springs up in the eyes of the fountain is definitely an attractive myth.

The springs of Jinan are pure and clear, just like the mood of the Jinan people; the springs of Jinan are not calm, and they are boiling, just like the enthusiasm of Jinan people. Traveling through these fountains, explanations are superfluous, and emotions are spilling over. Jinan is full of springs. It is not enough for you to visit here once. After you have seen them, if you quietly close your eyes, and you will be intoxicated. Sitting on the edge of the fountain, you will find it wonderful and heart-rending. Its beauty is full of tension. There are breathtaking mist on the surface of the fountain, which reveals the tranquility of Jinan culture. Listen, you can hear the rhythm of the life in this city and the silence before the prosperity.

Jinan City is full of springs. Jinan Street is filled with the aroma of springs. Jinan is full of spring charm. The city that emerges from the spring water has a variety of gorgeous postures and exotic beauty. The clear and luscious spring water nourishes Jinan and brings endless charm and inexhaustible connotations to the city.

Visiting such a city and appreciating its springs is definitely a pleasing thing.

So, just follow the lens of our mind and go to enjoy the emerging springs.

目录 Contents

Baotu Spring Group 趵突泉泉群

趵突泉	5	Baotu Spring
金线泉	8	Jinxian Spring
皇华泉	10	Huanghua Spring
柳絮泉	12	Liuxu Spring
卧牛泉	14	Woniu Spring
漱玉泉	16	Shuyu Spring
马跑泉	18	Mapao Spring
无忧泉	20	Wuyou Spring
石湾泉	22	Shiwan Spring
湛露泉	24	Zhanlu Spring
满井泉	26	Manjing Spring
登州泉	28	Dengzhou Spring
杜康泉	30	Dukang Spring
望水泉	32	Wangshui Spring

Zhenzhu Spring Group 珍珠泉泉群

珍珠泉	39	Zhenzhu Spring
散水泉	42	Sanshui Spring
溪亭泉	44	Xiting Spring
濯缨泉	46	Zhuoying Spring
芙蓉泉	48	Furong Spring
舜泉	50	Shun Spring
腾蛟泉	52	Tengjiao Spring

Heihu Spring Group 黑虎泉泉群

黑虎泉	59	Heihu Spring
琵琶泉	62	Pipa Spring
玛瑙泉	64	Manao Spring
白石泉	66	Baishi Spring
九女泉	68	Jiunyu Spring

五龙潭 泉群
Wulong Pond Spring Group

五龙潭	75	Wulong Pond
古温泉	78	Guwen Spring
贤清泉	80	Xianqing Spring
天镜泉	82	Tianjing Spring
月牙泉	84	Yueya Spring
西蜜脂泉	86	Ximizhi Spring
官家池	88	Guanjia Pond
回马泉	90	Huima Spring
虬溪泉	92	Qiuxi Spring
玉泉	94	Yu Spring
濂泉	96	Lian Spring

其他 名泉
Other Famous Springs

华泉	105	Hua Spring
甘露泉	108	Ganlu Spring
无影潭	110	Wuying Pond
涌泉	112	Yong Spring
避暑泉	114	Bishu Spring
圣水泉	116	Shengshui Spring
缎华泉	118	Duanhua Spring
百脉泉	120	Baimai Spring
东麻湾	122	Dongma Pond
墨泉	124	Mo Spring
梅花泉	126	Meihua Spring
净明泉	128	Jingming Spring
袈裟泉	130	Jiasha Spring
卓锡泉	132	Zhuoxi Spring
清泠泉	134	Qingling Spring
檀抱泉	136	Tanbao Spring
晓露泉	138	Xiaolu Spring
洪范池	140	Hongfan Pond
书院泉	142	Shuyuan Spring
扈泉	144	Hu Spring
日月泉	146	Riyue Spring

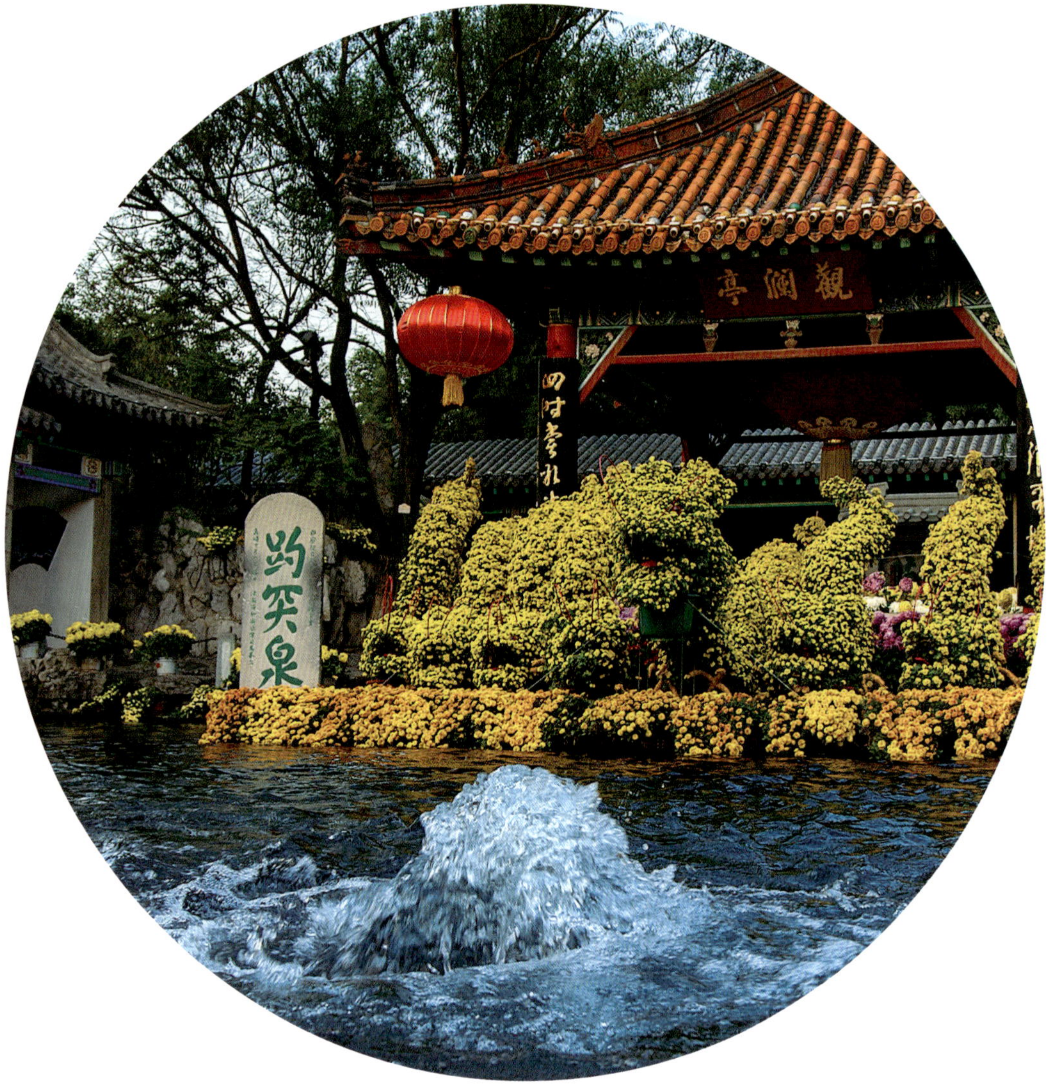
觀瀾亭
趵突泉

Baotu Spring Group

趵突泉

泉群

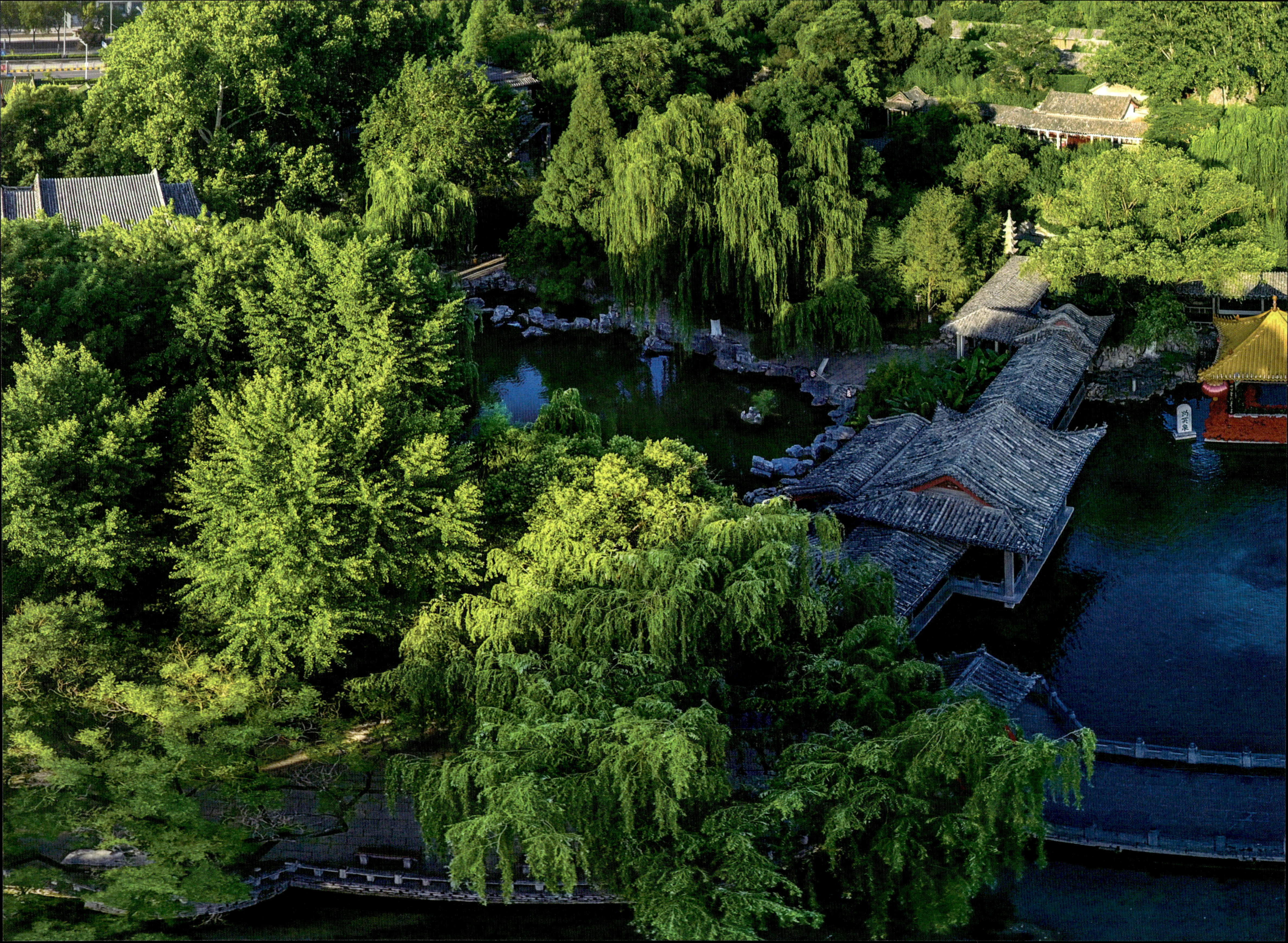

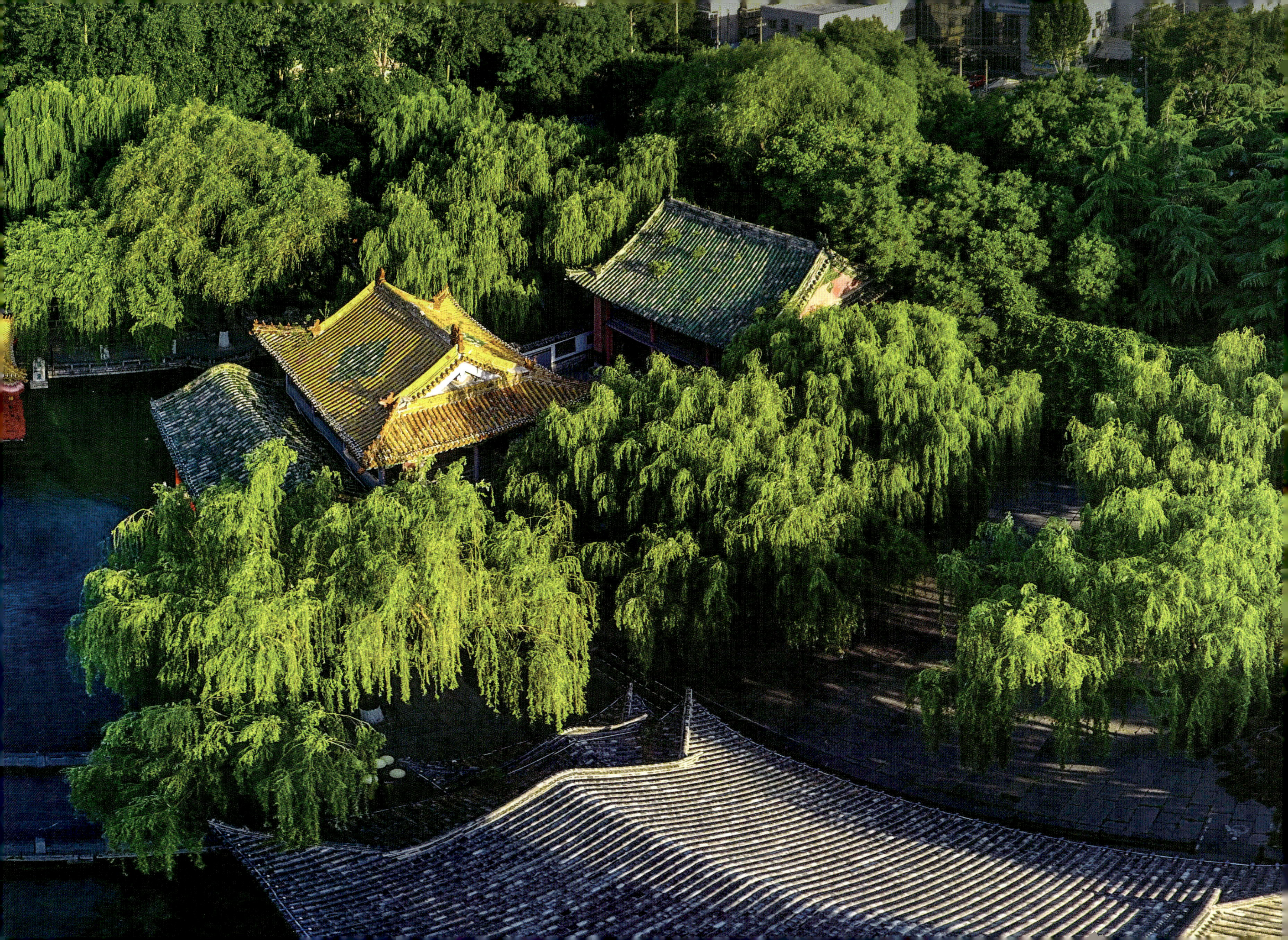

Baotu Spring Group

Baotu Spring Group locates in the southwest of old Jinan City. It is in the region from Baotu Spring South Road in the east to Yinhu Pond Street in the west, and from Luoyuan Street in the south to Gongqingtuan Road in the north. It is a 170,000m²-region which covers Baotu Spring Park and its surrounding areas. There are 31 springs, 28 of which are distributed in Baotu Spring Park. Among the 31 springs, 14 belong to the "Newly Selected 72 Famous Springs", namely, Baotu Spring, Jinxian Spring, Huanghua Spring, Liuxu Spring, Shuyu Spring, Woniu Spring, Manjing Spring, Mapao Spring, Wuyou Spring, Shiwan Spring, Zhanlu Spring, Dengzhou Spring, Dukang Spring, and Wangshui Spring. The others are Old Jinxian Spring, Qianjing Spring, Xibo Spring, Hunsha Spring, Jiu Spring, Donggao Spring, Luowen Spring, Shangzhi Spring, Cang Sping, Huaqiangzi Spring, Baiyun Spring, Quanting Pond, Bailong Pond, and Yinhu Pond.

趵突泉泉群

趵突泉泉群位于济南老城西南，东起趵突泉南路，西至饮虎池街，南临泺源大街，北靠共青团路，分布面积约170 000平方米，共有泉眼31处，其中28处集中分布在趵突泉公园内。该泉群中属于"新七十二名泉"的有：趵突泉、金线泉、皇华泉、柳絮泉、漱玉泉、卧牛泉、满井泉、马跑泉、无忧泉、石湾泉、湛露泉、登州泉、杜康泉、望水泉等14处。其他还有老金线泉、浅井泉、洗钵泉、混沙泉、酒泉、东高泉、螺纹泉、尚志泉、沧泉、花墙子泉、白云泉、泉亭池、白龙湾、饮虎池等。

趵突泉

泺水发源天下无，
平地涌出白玉壶。
谷虚久恐元气泄，
岁旱不愁东海枯。
云雾润蒸华不注，
波澜声震大明湖。
时来泉上濯尘土，
冰雪满怀清兴孤。

（元）赵孟頫《趵突泉》

趵突泉有文字记载的历史，可上溯到3500多年前。该泉因盛水期时"跳沫涌轮数尺许"而得名。趵，跳跃也。突，高于周围也。"其水自三穴中涌出，各高二三尺。怒起跃突，如三柱鼎立，并势争高，不肯相下。"（清·怀应聘《游趵突泉记》）该泉位于趵突泉公园内的泺源堂前，观澜亭东。

Baotu Spring

The written record of Baotu Spring dates back to about 3,500 years ago. It was named for its jumping foams which can reach inches high when its water is abundant. Bao, means "jump"; tu, means "higher than its surroundings". "Three gushes of water are jumping two-or-three inches high, just like three columns erecting and competing to be the highest"(Huai Yingpin, Qing Dynasty, *A Record of Baotu Spring*). It is in front of Luoyuan Hall and to the east of Guanlan Pavilion in Baotu Spring Park.

Jinan:
A City Enriched by Famous Springs

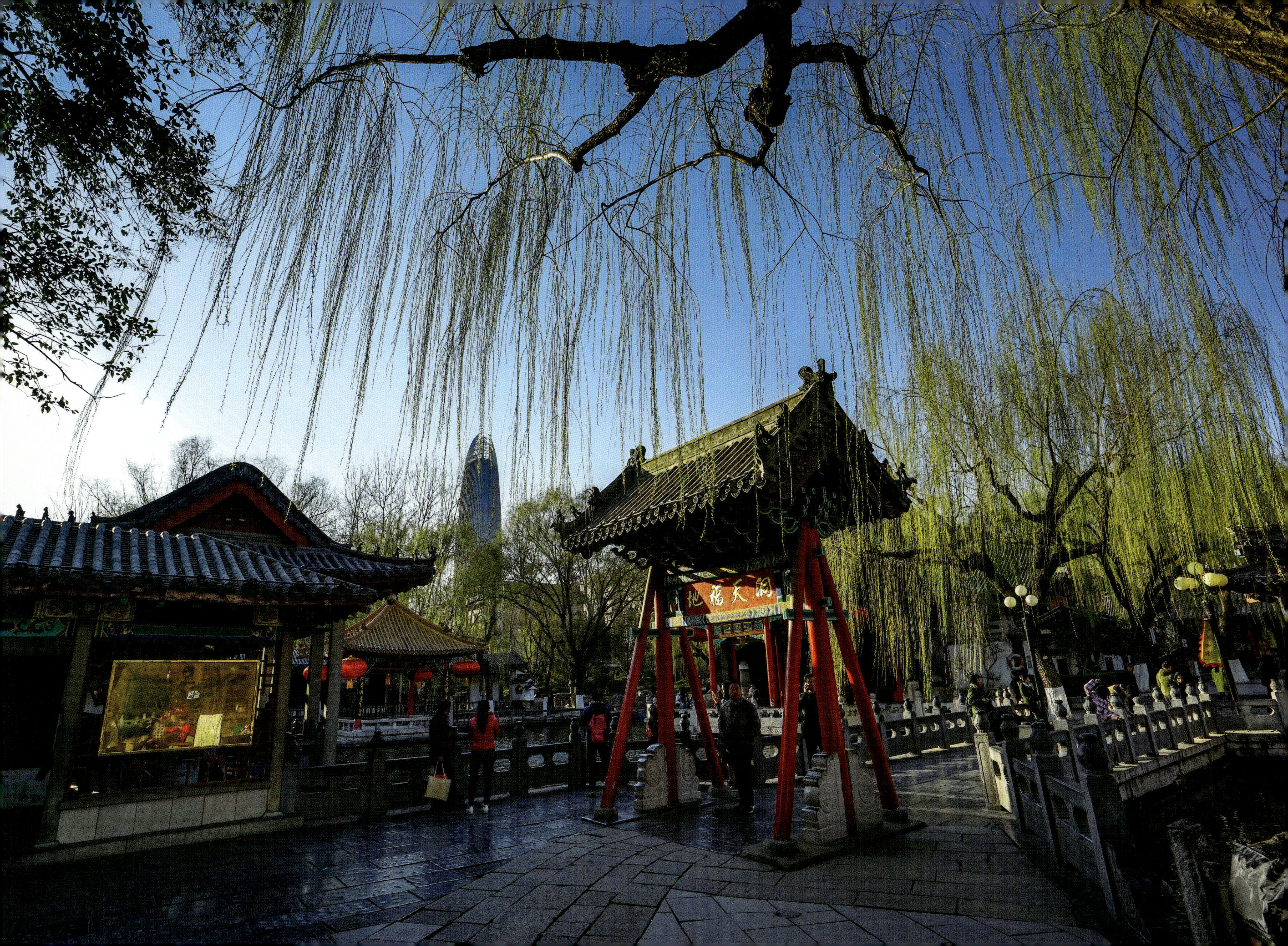
洞天福地

水纹浮绿影摇金，
倒挽银河百尺深。
中有锦鳞三十六，
碧波荡漾任浮沉。
〔明〕晏璧《济南七十二泉诗》

Jinxian Spring

It is a famous and quaint spring. Two gushes of water spews from the east and south walls of the spring pool, merging into one streak and twinkling under the sun like a golden (*jin*) thread (*xian*). That is why it is so called. It is to the south of Liuxu Spring in Baotu Spring Park.

金线泉

该泉是一著名奇泉，泉池东壁、南壁各有泉水流出，两股泉水相拥，聚成一条水纹漂浮移动，在光线映照下，如同一条闪耀的金线，因此得名"金线泉"。泉池位于趵突泉公园内，柳絮泉南侧。

金线泉

皇华泉

皇华泉之名出自《诗经·皇皇者华》，"皇华"字面意思是"艳丽的鲜花"，暗用使臣访贤求策、不辱君命的典故，指该泉的风采就像皇帝的使者，辉煌华丽，光彩夺目。该泉为渗流泉，水自池底沙际渗出，常年不竭。泉池位于趵突泉公园内的皇华轩南面东侧，柳絮泉西。

Huanghua Spring

Its name is derived from the *Book of Songs*. The literal meaning of "huanghua" is "charming flowers". Here it alludes to the story of an envoy who accomplished his mission of visiting the wise and asking for advice. The charm of this spring is just like that of the envoy, which is glorious and gorgeous. The water exudates inexhaustibly from the bottom of the pool year after year. It is to the southeast of Huanghua House and to the west of Liuxu Spring in Baotu Spring Park.

金线池东涌碧泉，皇华使节耀齐川。
圣恩浩荡宽如海，散作甘霖遍八埏。
〔明〕晏璧《济南七十二泉诗》

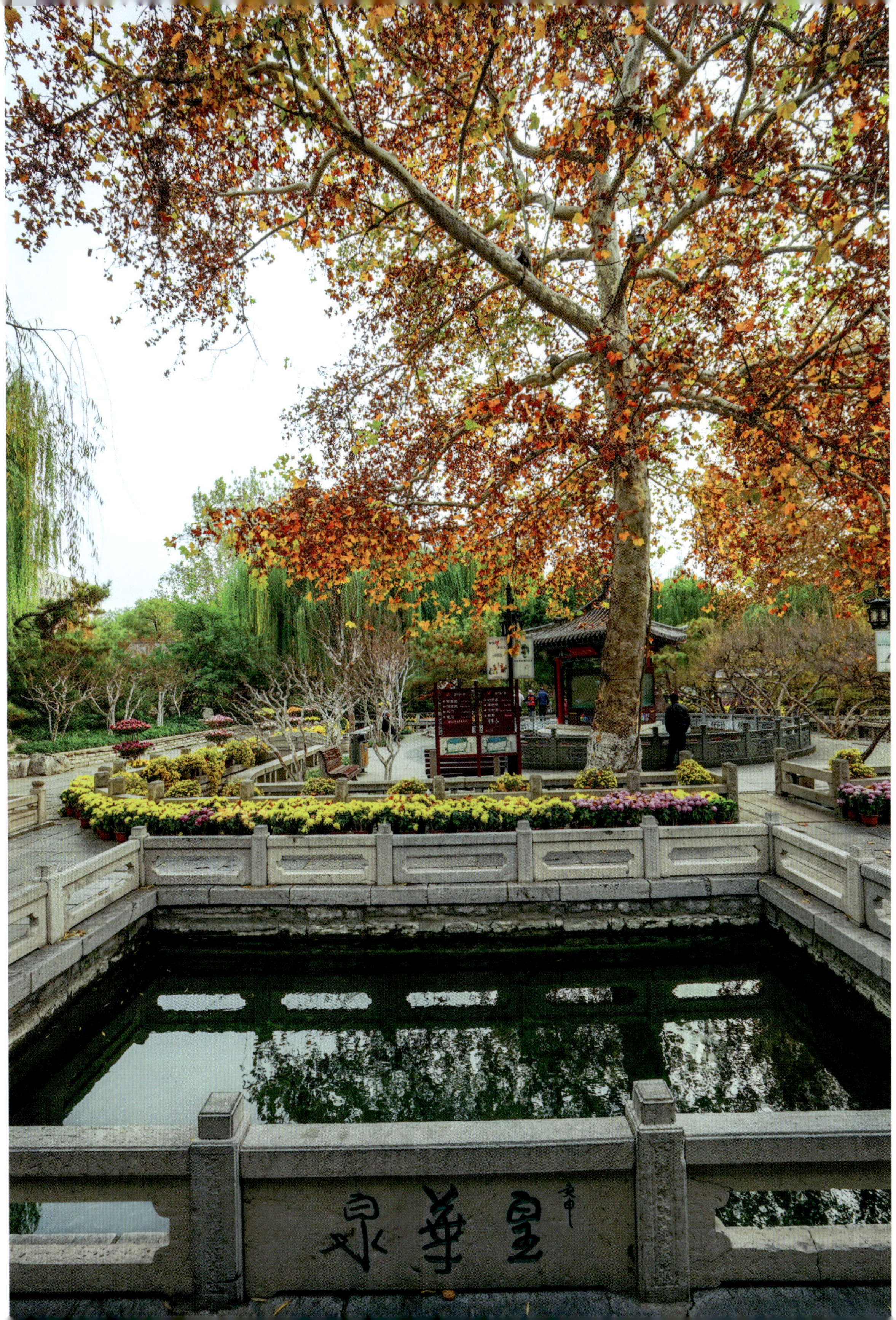
皇華泉
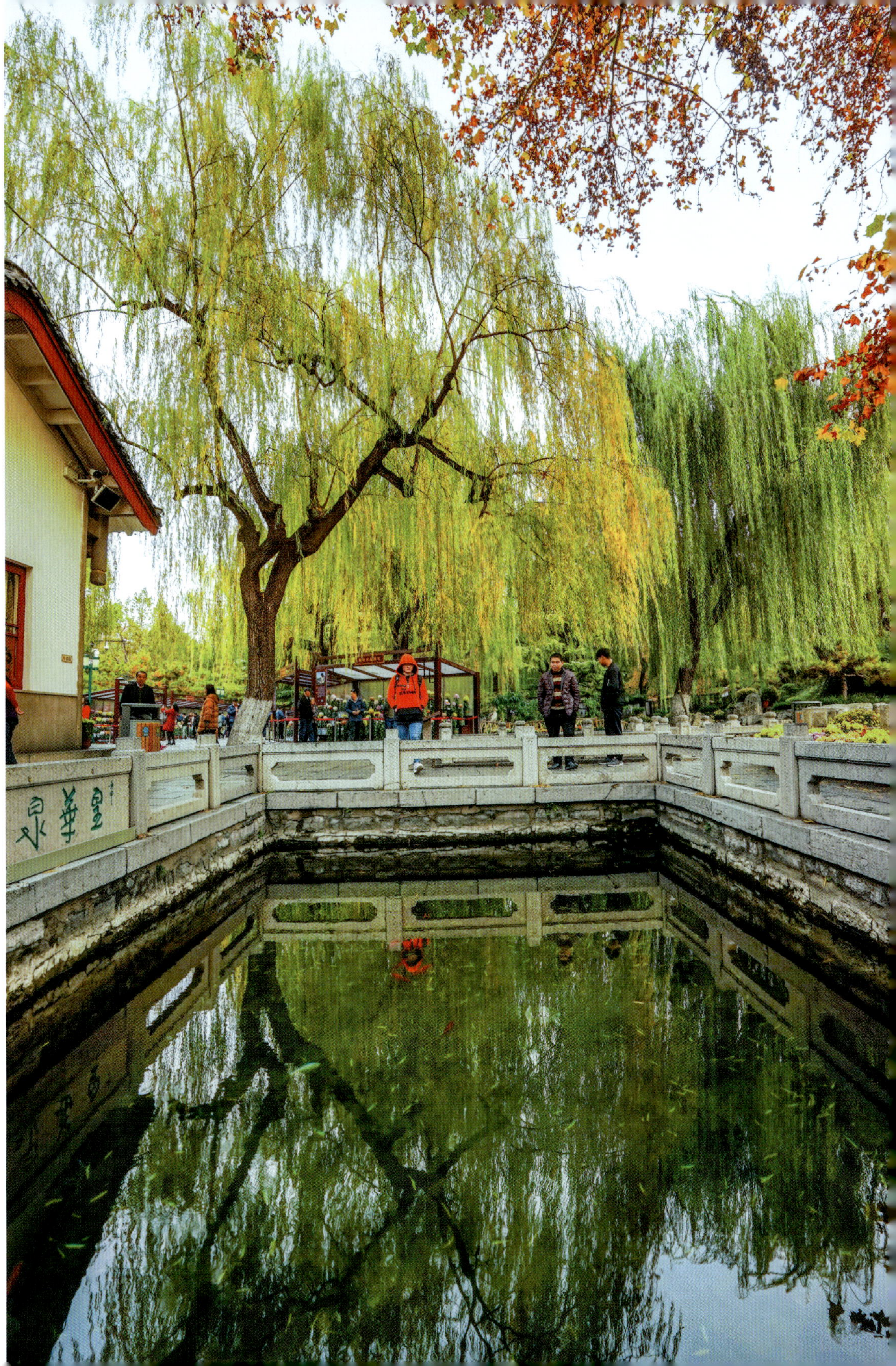
皇華泉

Liuxu Spring

The spring pool is surrounded by several weeping willows. Every spring, the willow catkins fly around while the clear water reflects their lightness. Meanwhile, the water foams up like the flying catkins, so it is called Liuxu (catkins). It is said that the famous poetess Li Qingzhao of the Song Dynasty used to live beside this spring. The Li Qingzhao Memorial Hall and her former residence are to the north of the spring. It is to the north of Jinxian Spring and to the east of Huanghua Spring in Baotu Spring Park.

柳絮泉

该泉泉池四周植有垂柳多株，每到阳春三月，柳絮纷飞，清泉倒映，流光溢彩，春色无限，加之池内"泉沫纷翻，如絮飞舞"，故名"柳絮泉"。相传，宋代女词人李清照曾在泉畔居住，今泉北建有李清照纪念堂和易安故居。泉池位于趵突泉公园内的金线泉以北，皇华泉以东。

金线池边杨柳青，
泉分石窦晓泠泠。
东风三月飘香絮，
一夜随波化绿萍。
〔明〕晏璧《济南七十二泉诗》

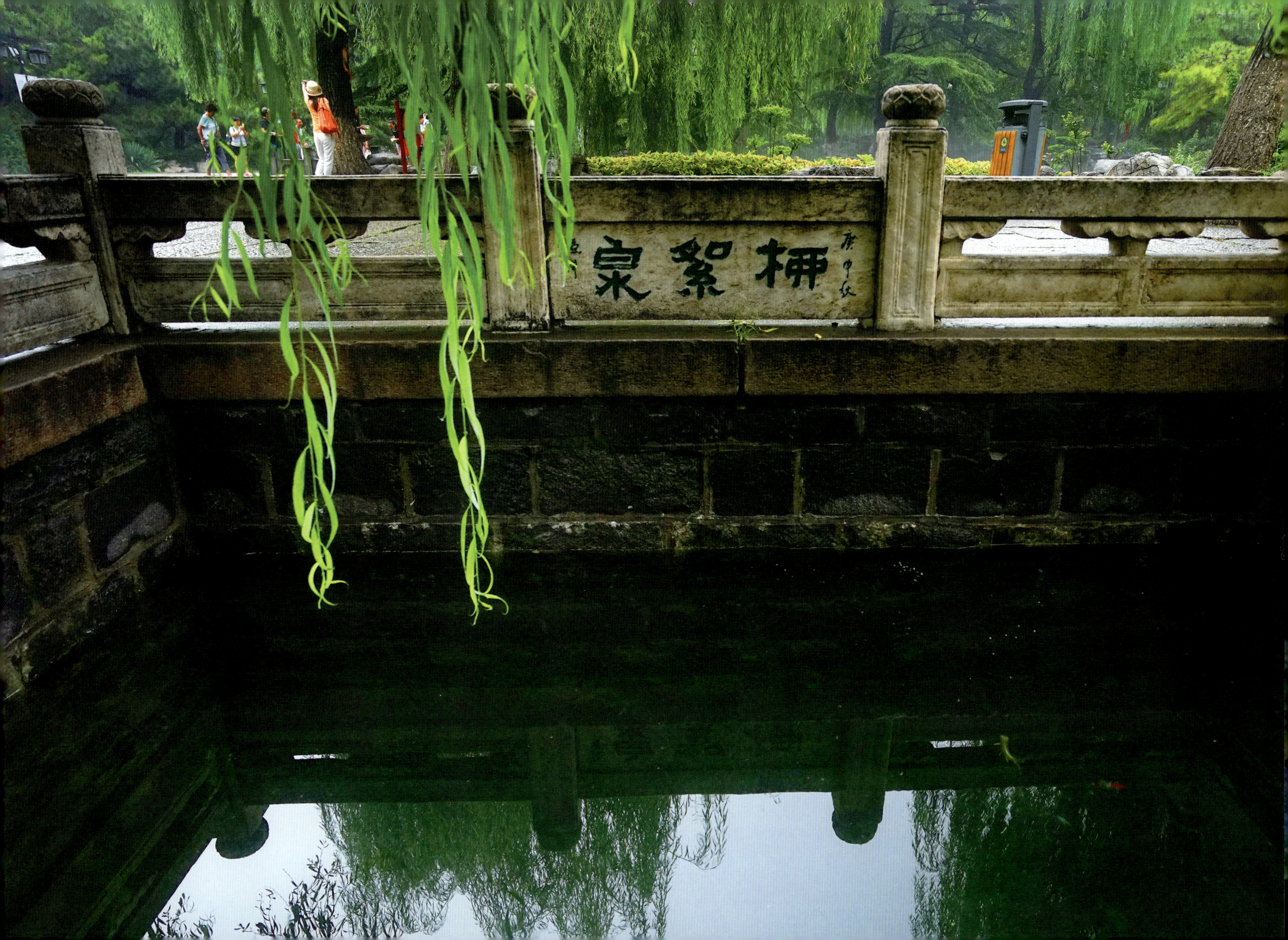
柳絮泉

昔闻陶墓有牛眠，今见齐州溢井泉。千载历山遗胜迹，秋风禾黍满虞田。

〔明〕晏璧《济南七十二泉诗》

卧牛泉

古时，卧牛泉一带还是一片田园风光，常有牛羊在此饮水，并卧在泉旁休息，故而得名"卧牛泉"。该泉晶莹碧透，水质清冽，位于趵突泉公园内的皇华轩南面西侧，东与皇华泉相对。

Woniu Spring

In ancient times, the area surrounding Woniu Spring was countryside. Cattle and goats often drank its water and rested beside it. Therefore, the spring was named Woniu (lying cattle). The spring is crystal-clear and its water is clean and cool. It is to the southwest of Huanghua House and opposite Huanghua Spring in Baotu Spring Park.

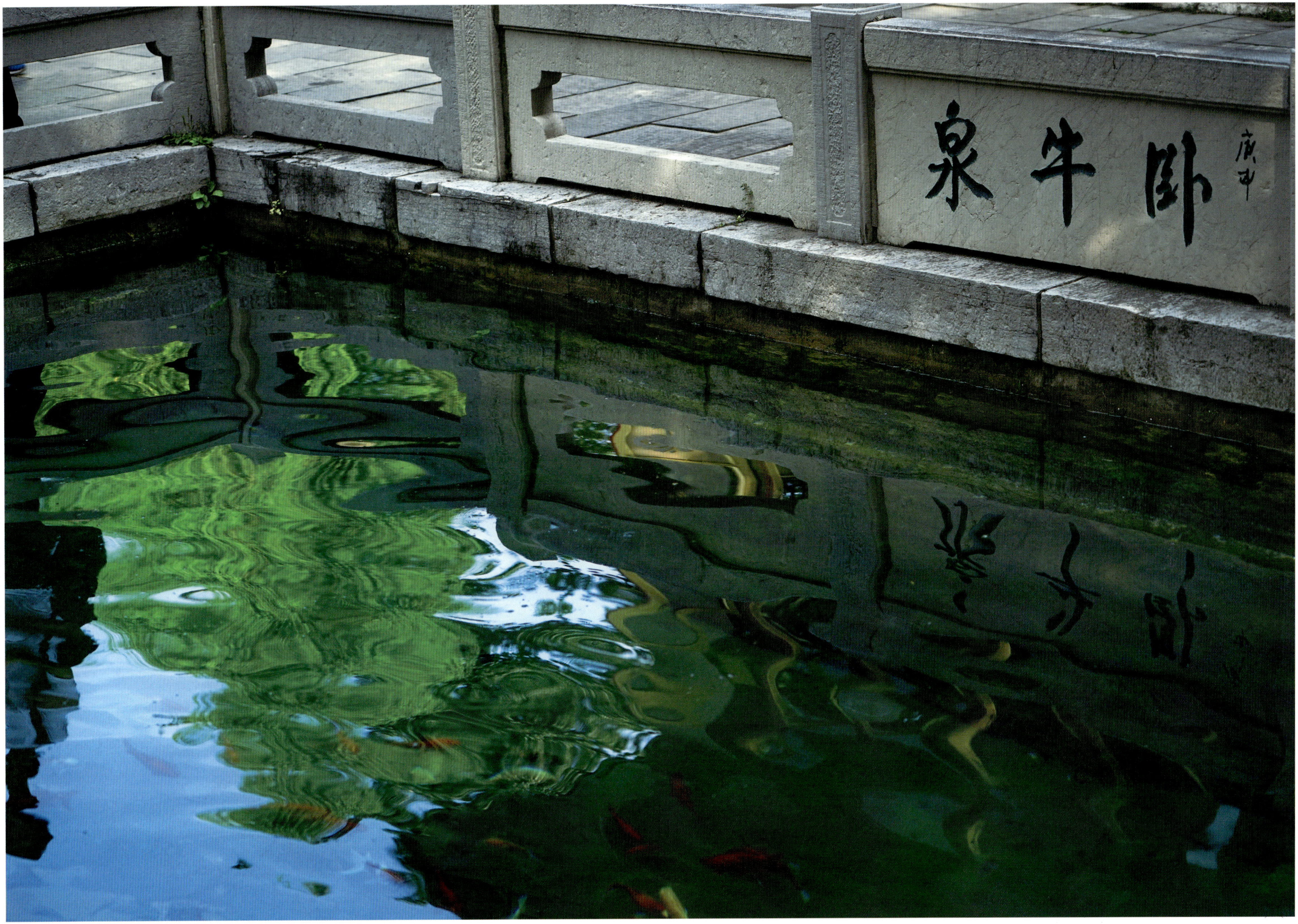
卧牛泉
庚申

漱玉泉

　　漱玉，谓泉流漱石，声若击玉。宋代女词人李清照有《漱玉集》传世，此泉故得名"漱玉泉"。泉水自池底涌出，形成水泡，漂浮至水面破裂，咝咝作响，然后漫石穿隙，层叠而下，声响犹如击打玉石一般。该泉位于趵突泉公园内的李清照纪念堂南，柳絮泉东。

Shuyu Spring

Shuyu, means "the water scours the stones, creating a sound like knocking on the jade". It is so called because the poetess Li Qingzhao's anthology was also titled Shuyu. The water gushes from the bottom of the spring pool and produces many bubbles. The spring with bubbles floats to the surface and pops, creating penetrating vibrations that go through the stones, and it sounds like knocking on the jade. It is to the south of Li Qingzhao Memorial Hall and to the east of Liuxu Spring in Baotu Spring Park.

南泉漱玉派匡庐,
应是云门瀑布余。
月照波心清可鉴,
岂无湘女解琼琚。

〔明〕晏璧《济南七十二泉诗》

马跑泉

据《宋史》《金史》记载，北宋末年，济南武将关胜多次出城抗御金兵，终被济南知府、后来的伪齐皇帝刘豫杀害。相传，关胜的坐骑见主人遇难，怒吼咆哮，愤而刨地，竟然刨出一眼清泉。为纪念关胜这位民族英雄，人们遂把该泉命名为"马刨泉"，后因谐音而被传为"马跑泉"。此泉位于趵突泉公园内的李清照纪念堂东面，假山西北侧。

Mapao Spring

According to the *History of Song* and the *History of Jin*, in the last years of the Northern Song Dynasty, a general named Guan Sheng, who was in charge of the defense of Jinan, battled bravely against the Jin army. Finally, he was betrayed and killed by Jinan Administer later the ruler of the puppet government, Liu Yu. It's said that Guan Sheng's horse was so sorrowful and indignant that it dug the ground furiously. It was amazing that a spring of water flushed out. In order to memorize the patriotic hero, people named the spring Mapao (ma, means "horse"; pao, means "dig"). It is to the east of Li Qingzhao Memorial Hall and to the northwest of the rockworks.

将军战马就悬崖，石底空闻吼怒雷。
四铁一敲冰雪涌，始知赤兔本龙媒。
（明）王象春《马跑泉》

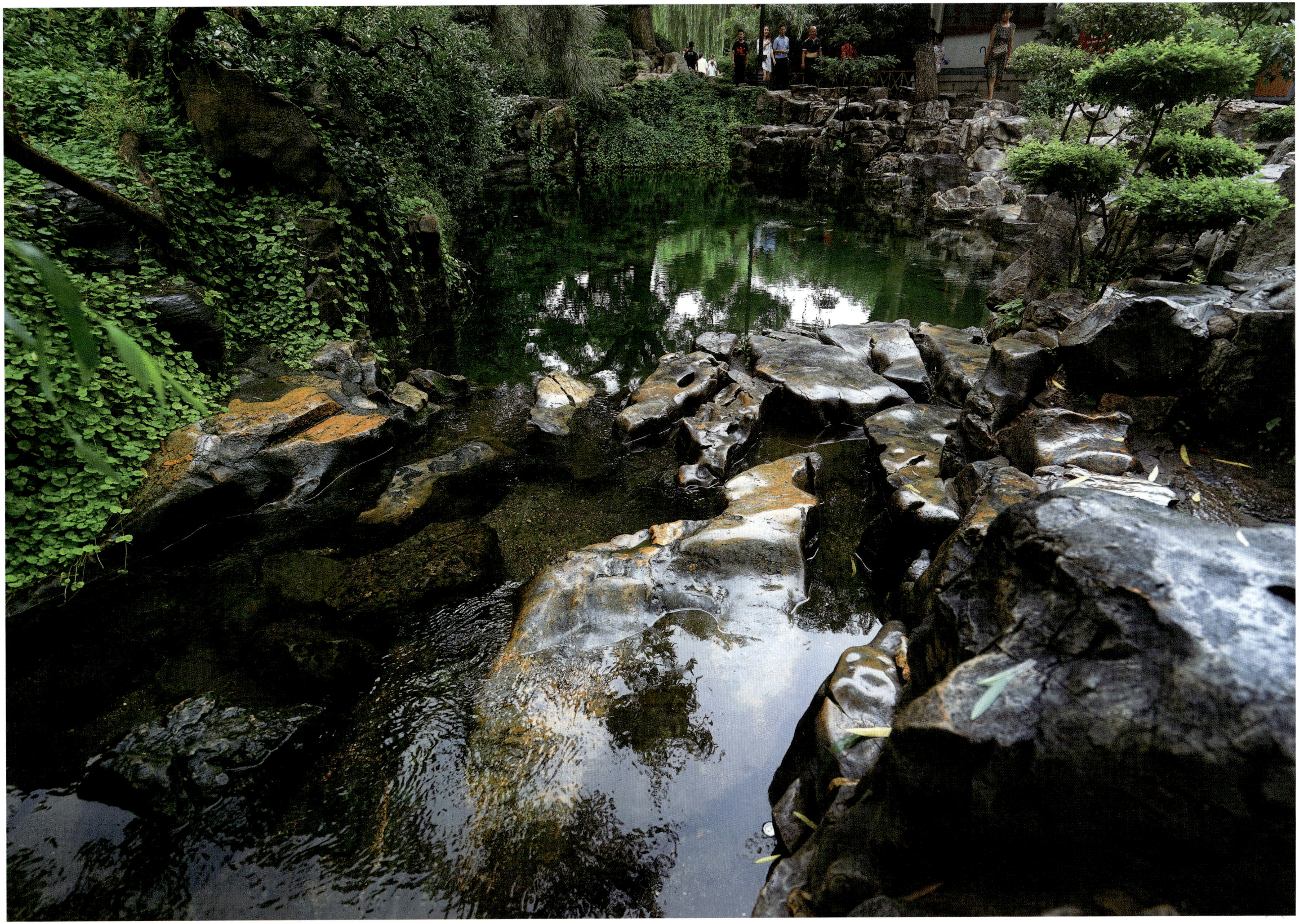

槛泉西畔漱清流,
酌水能消万斛愁。
白叟黄童争击壤,
春来有事向东畴。

〔明〕晏璧《济南七十二泉诗》

无忧泉

传说饮用此泉泉水后,能使人解忧消愁、心情舒畅,此泉故而得名"无忧泉"。泉池内锦鲤游逐,碧水盈盈;泉畔杨柳垂荫,修竹摇曳,是观赏、休憩的好去处。泉池位于白雪楼西北,南临趵突泉。

Wuyou Spring

It is said that anyone who drink its water will forget all his worries and sorrows and enjoys ease of mind, so this spring is called Wuyou (carefree). Beautiful koi fishes are swimming in it; willows and bamboos are surrounding it. It is a good place to visit and take a rest. It is to the northwest of Snow Building and to the north of Baotu Spring.

无忧泉

Shiwan Spring

The spring was named Shiwan because it is accompanied by big rocks (*shi*) on its edge, and looks like an inlet (*wan*). Shiwan Spring has long been famous since the Jin Dynasty, which is more than 900 years ago. In ancient times, its water was clean and sweet, and perfect for making tea. The water was even comparable to that of Baotu Spring. Nowadays, it is surrounded by grotesque rocks and lush trees; its water is still clear and lotuses are fully planted in it. It is to the south of Snow Building and to the north of the rockworks inside the south gate of Baotu Spring Park.

石湾地接槛泉南,
涌出清流味更甘。
旋汲井花烹石鼎,
崝华秋净幕烟涵。
(明)晏璧《济南七十二泉诗》

石湾泉

石湾泉,因池边巨石驳岸、状如水湾而得名,在900多年前的金代,此泉就已赫赫有名。古时的石湾泉水,色清味甘,煮茗添香,水质堪与趵突泉相比。如今,石湾泉边怪石嶙峋,花木葱茏;池内泉水清澈,遍植莲荷。泉址位于趵突泉公园南门内假山北面,白雪楼南。

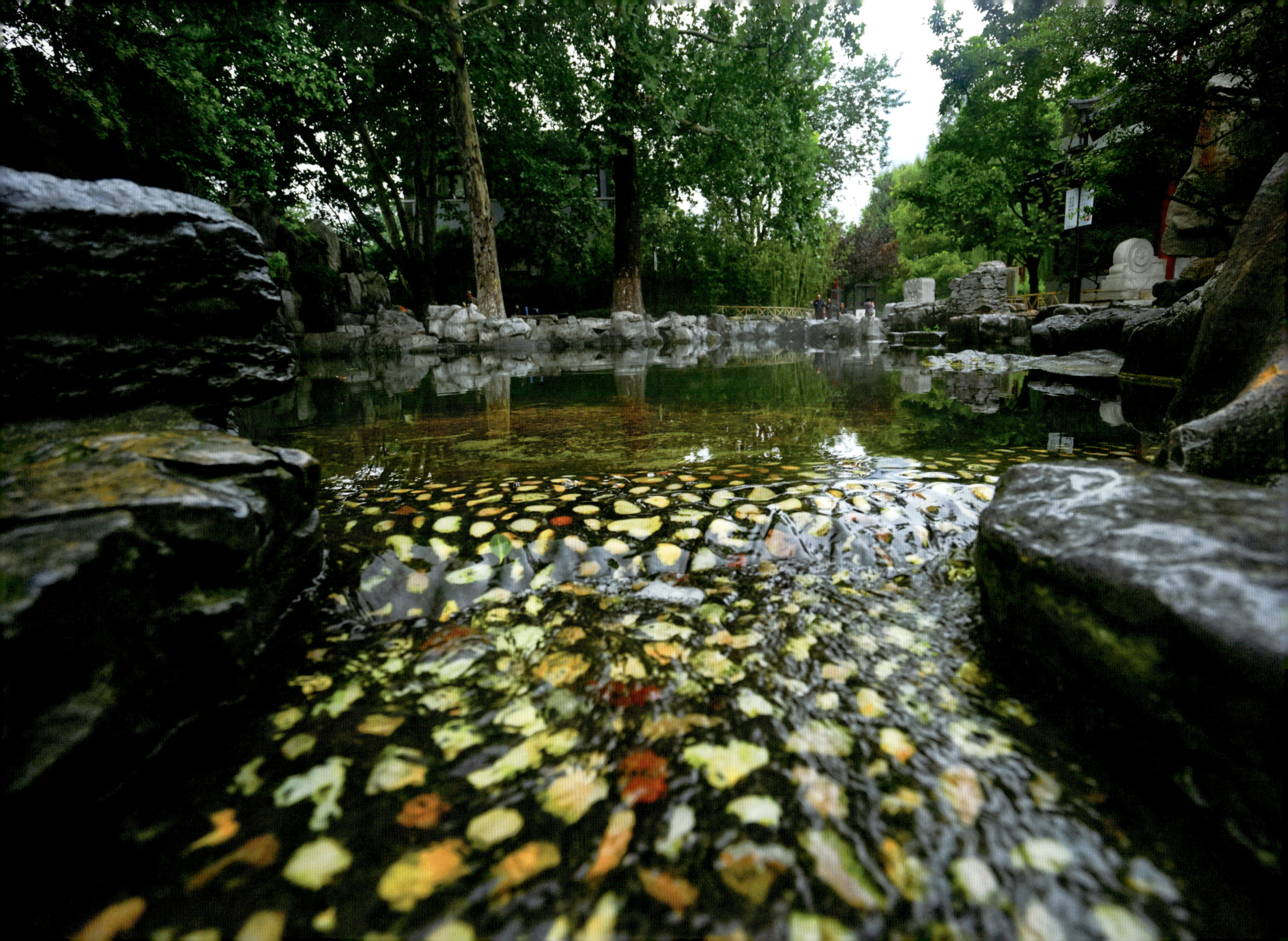

泉如湛露味甘香，
润入三焦齿颊凉。
通乐古园饶爽气，
厌厌夜饮醉无妨。
〔明〕晏璧《济南七十二泉诗》

Zhanlu Spring

Its name is derived from the poem "Zhanlu" of the *Book of Songs*. Zhanlu, means "thick morning dew". This poem was also the song performed when the emperor feasted the dukes and princes. There is a sentence in it which means "In such a luxurious feast, nobody can go home unless he is drunk". Therefore, Zhanlu is used here as a metaphor of heavenly benefit. Its water is considered as tasty as alcohol. It is to the southwest of Snow Building and to the northwest of the rockworks inside the south gate of Baotu Spring Park.

湛露泉

泉名出自《诗经·湛露》，"湛露"指晨露又浓又重。《湛露》诗也是天子宴请诸侯时演奏的乐曲，诗中有"厌厌夜饮，不醉无归"之句。湛露泉以"湛露"喻上天恩泽，又因泉水淙淙、味香如酒而名。该泉位于趵突泉公园南门内假山西北，白雪楼西南。

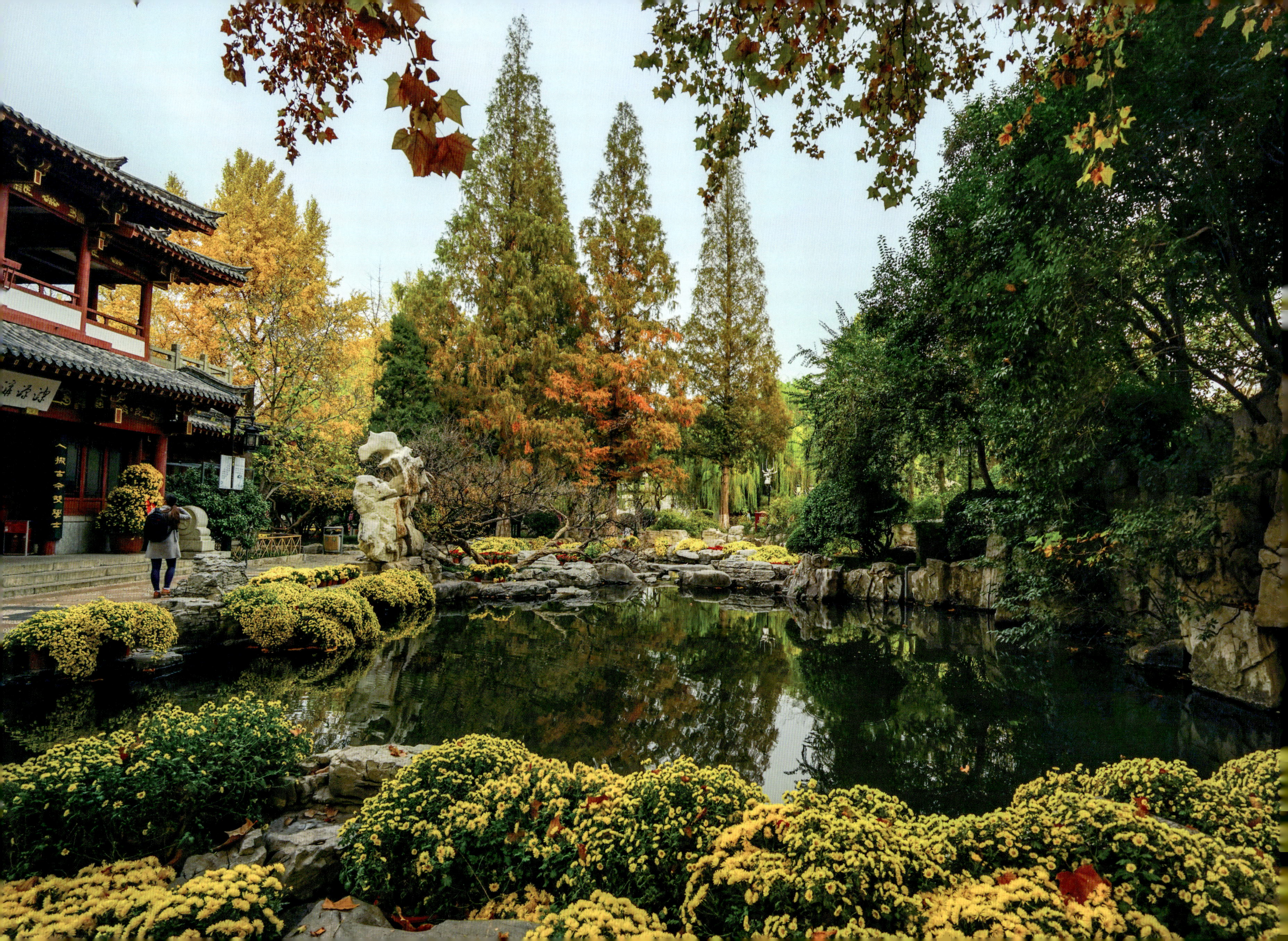

满井泉

泉名因丰水期泉水可溢出池口、清可鉴人而得。泉池呈六边形，甃以石砌而成，池周饰以雕石栏杆，现位于趵突泉公园内的趵突泉北，三圣殿西南隅，娥英祠北墙后。

Manjing Spring

It is so called because its abundant water can overflow the pool side and reflect people as a mirror. The pool is in a shape of hexagon, and its walls are made of stone. The well is surrounded by carved stone rails. It is to the north of Baotu Spring, to the southwest of Sansheng Temple and behind the north wall of Eying Temple.

凡物盈则亏，尔泉盍自警。不见学道人，终日羞短绠。

（清）张菁恒《满井泉》

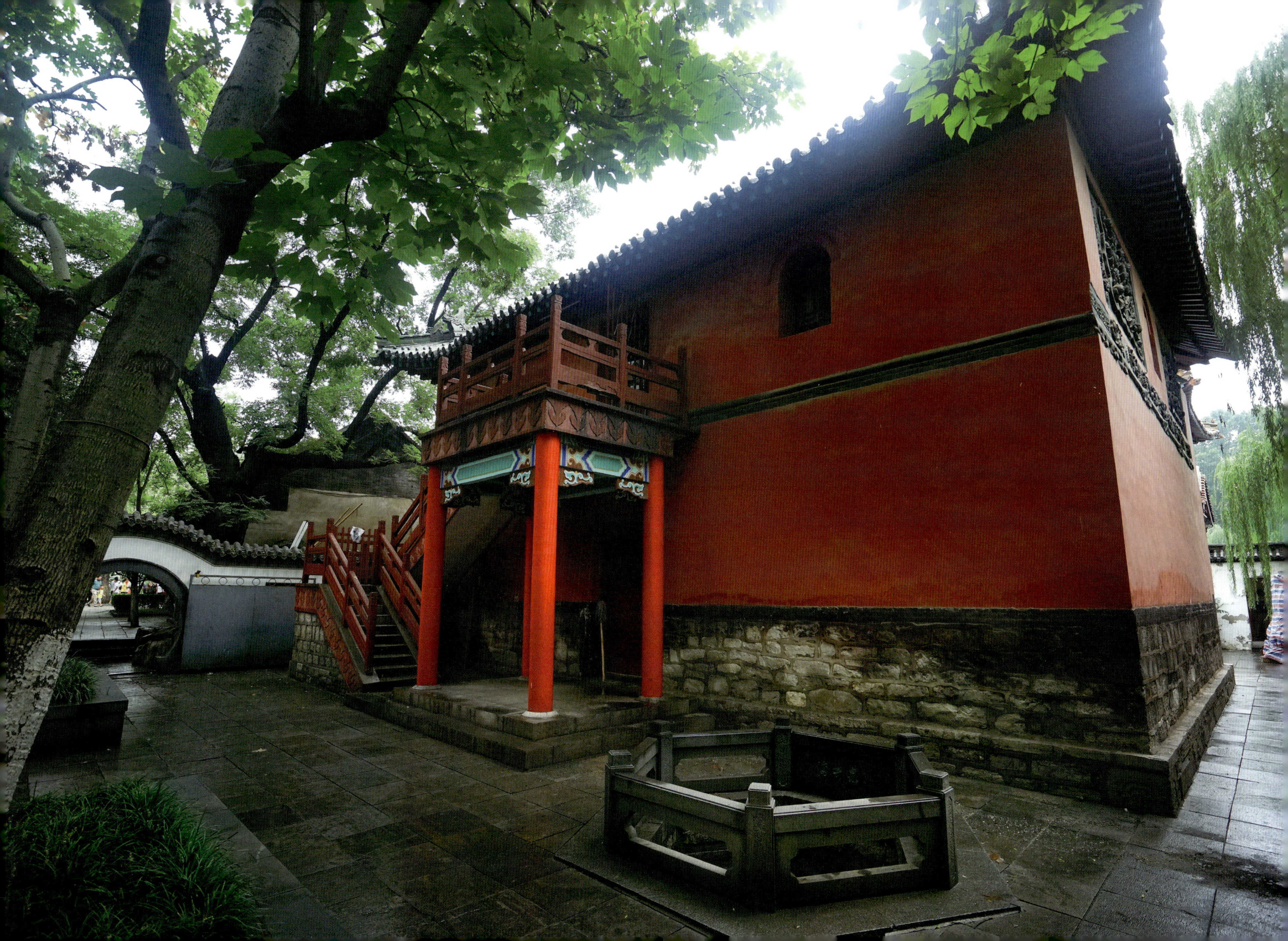

Dengzhou Spring

It is said that its water is connected with that of Dengzhou, which is the east end of Shandong Peninsula and thousand miles away. That is to say, its water comes all the way from Dengzhou. In fact, just like Baotu Spring, Dengzhou Spring is from the underground water of Southern Mountain Area of Jinan. It is to the west of Baotu Spring and to the south of Dukang Spring.

登州泉

传说此泉因与距其千里之遥、地处山东半岛最东端的登州水脉相连，故而得名。实际上，登州泉的泉脉同趵突泉一样，都是从济南南部山区潜流而来。此泉位于趵突泉公园内的趵突泉以西，杜康泉以南。

文登一脉透潭城,
澄澈全无蛊气腥。
安得雪堂苏学士,
朗吟万竹濯清泠。

(明)晏璧《济南七十二泉诗》

杜康泉（北煮糠泉）

明代以前，杜康泉被称为"北煮糠泉"。因何煮糠？盖因造酒也。因"煮糠"与古代造酒鼻祖杜康之名谐音，遂被讹称为"杜康泉"；又因老城刷律巷内另有一处"杜康泉"，故该泉被命名为"广会杜康泉"。如今，另一"杜康泉"已失，唯一的"杜康泉"就在此了。此泉位于趵突泉公园内的观澜桥以西，登州泉以北。

Dukang Spring (Beizhukang Spring)

Before the Ming Dynasty, Dukang Spring was called Beizhukang Spring. "Zhukang" means "making wine". "Zhukang" is similar in pronunciation with "Du Kang", the ancient originator of wine-making, so it was falsely called Dukang on purpose. It was once called Guanghui Dukang Spring because there was another Dukang Spring in the Shualyu Lane of the old city. Nowadays, the other one has disappeared, so the only Dukang Spring remains here. It is to the west of Guanlan Bridge and to the north of Dengzhou Spring in Baotu Spring Park.

杜郎去已远，泉仍留其名。
我来俯一掬，顿觉吟眸明。
我来饮一勺，能使枯肠清。
渴欲狂饮之，一酿千日醒。
鸿也高阳徒，陶然有真情。
忧至何以解，醉处访先生。

（清）王鸿 见《啸月楼诗录》

望水名泉古碣传，
浅深水旱好占年。
若因甲乙排名次，
洗钵应称廿五泉。
（清·范坰《望水泉》）

Wangshui Spring

It is said that in ancient times, there was a Wangshui (watch the water) tree (Dalbergia Hupeana) beside this spring. This kind of tree sprouts in the end of spring. Ancient people thought the flourishing and withering of its leaves could be used to predict the rising and falling of the water level, so the spring was named Wangshui. It is located in Wanzhu Garden of Baotu Spring Park.

望水泉

　　古时该泉泉畔植有一株望水檀（即黄檀），每到春末夏初才绽露新芽。古人认为，此树树叶的枯荣和望水泉水的枯丰在节令上十分契合，以此可判断泉水的涌量，遂将该泉命名为"望水泉"。泉池现位于趵突泉公园的万竹园内。

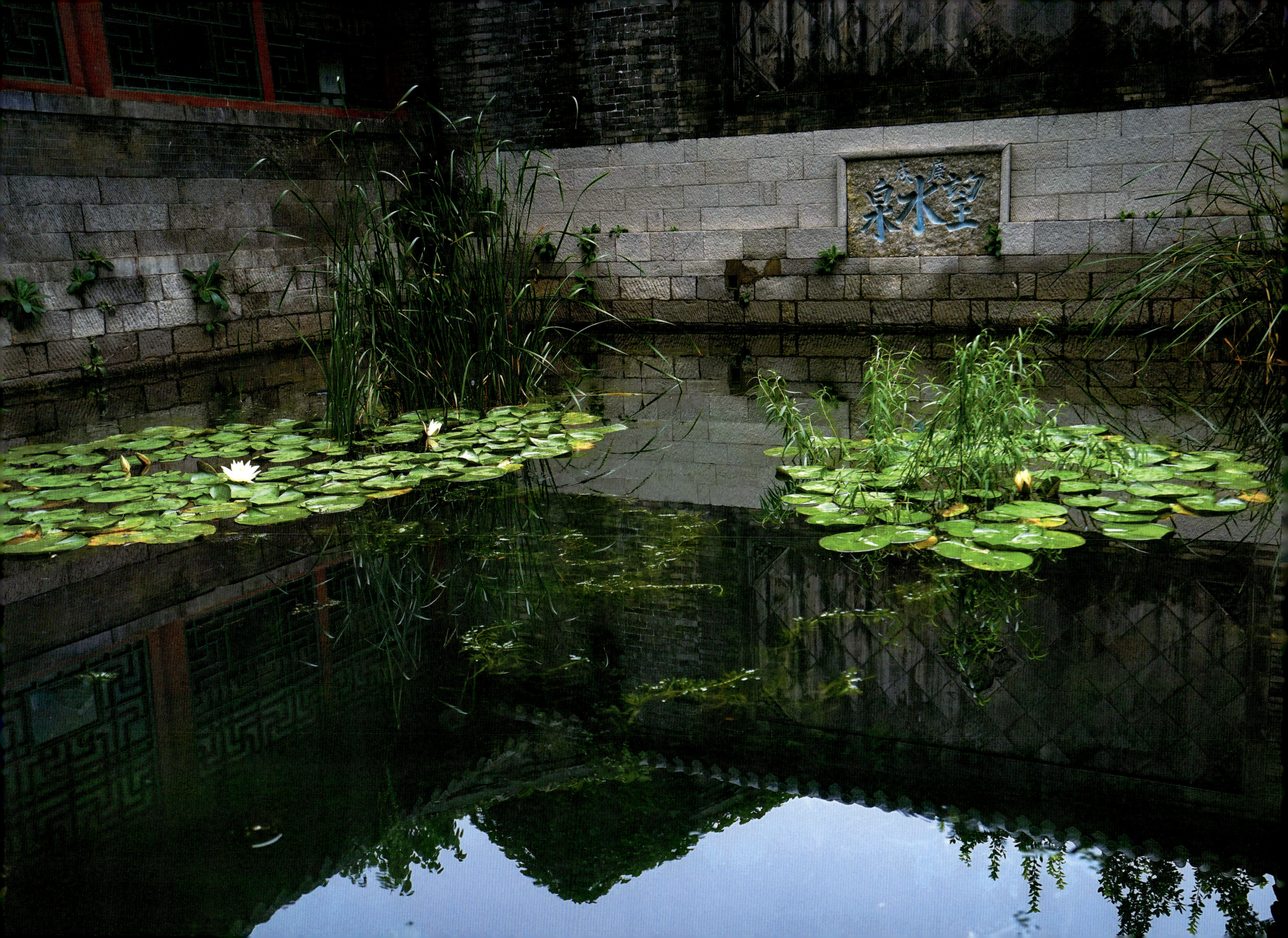
望水泉

Jinan:
A City Enriched by
Famous Springs

Zhenzhu Spring Group

珍珠泉

泉群

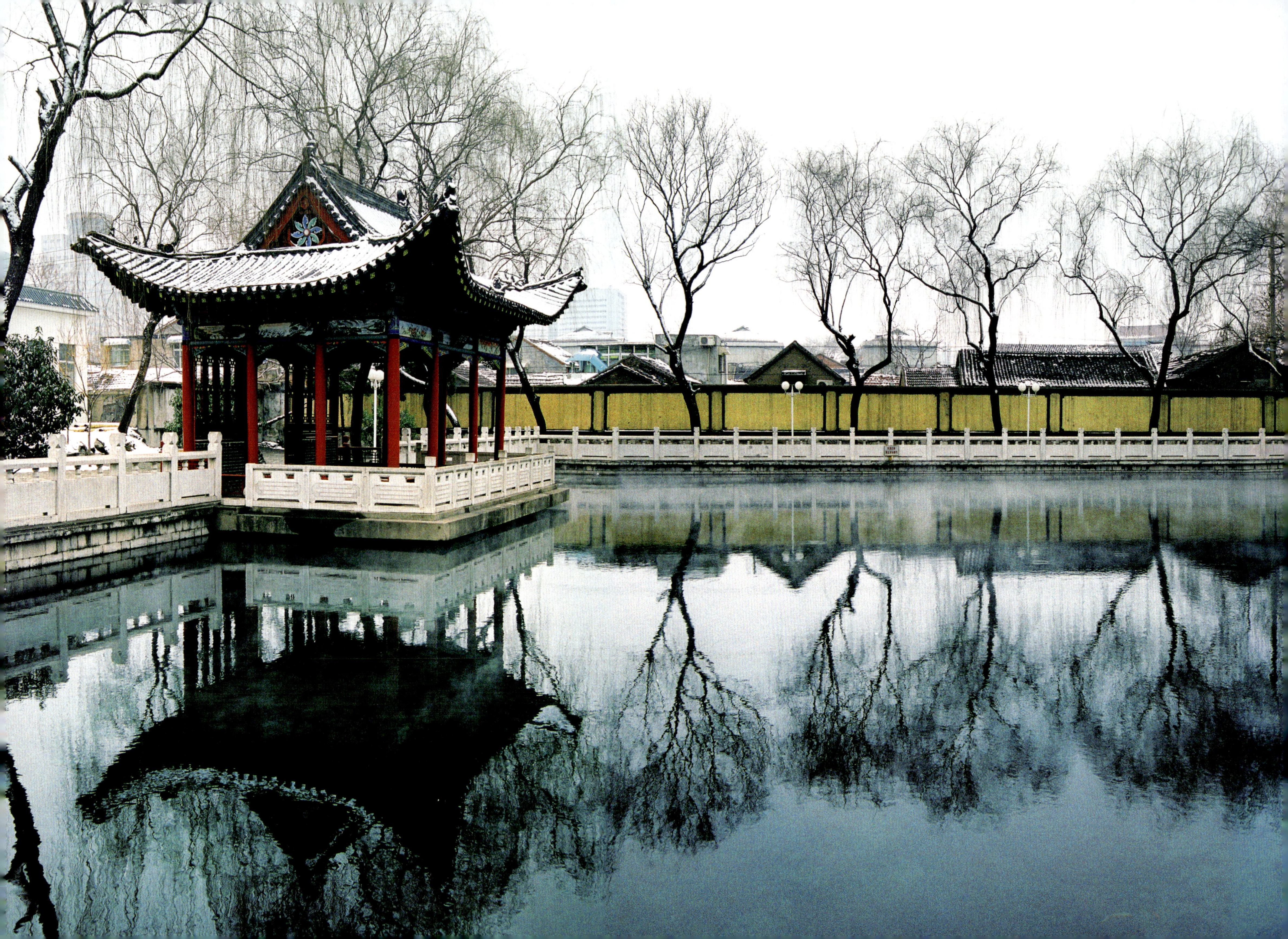

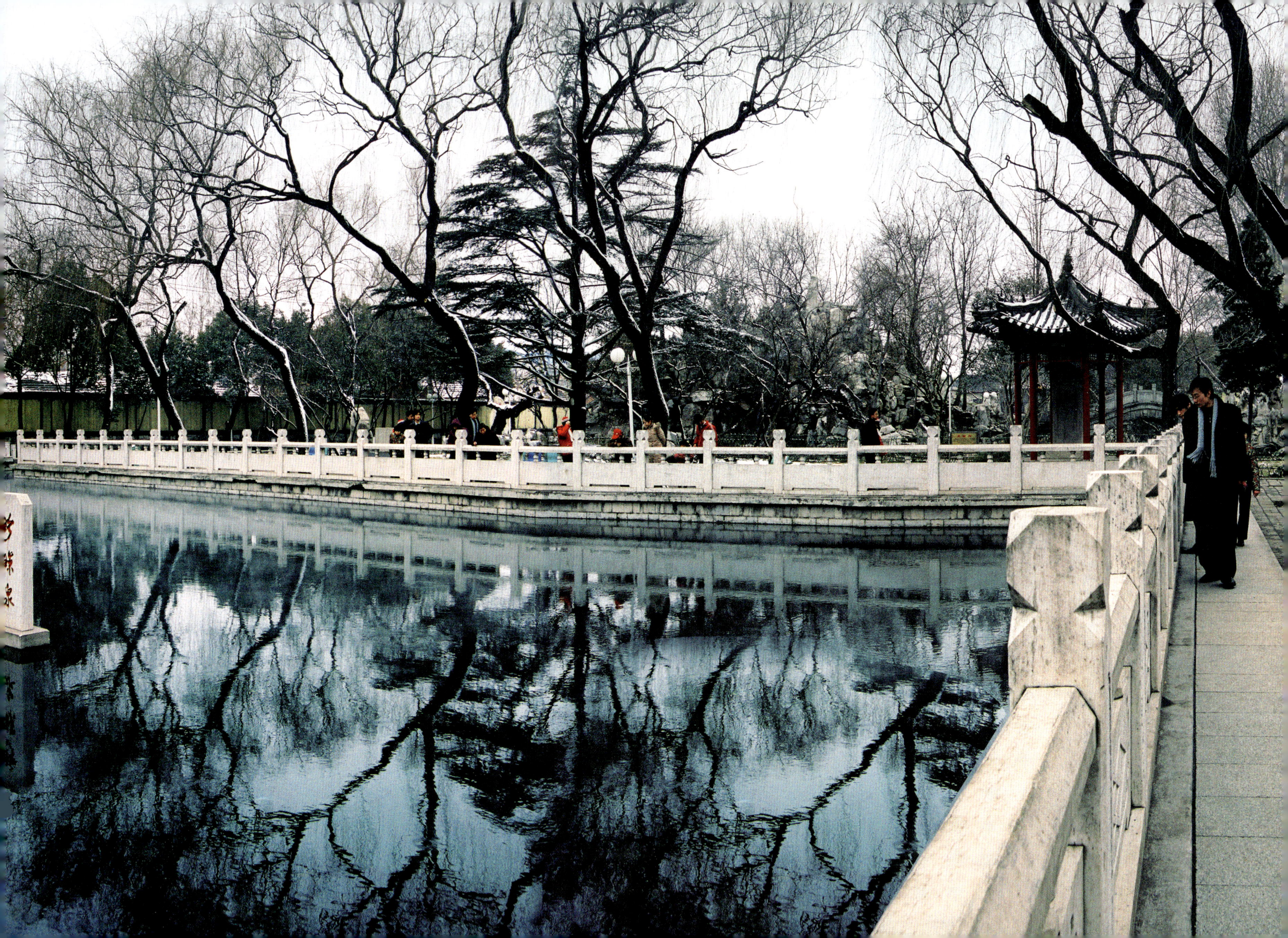
珍珠泉

Zhenzhu Spring Group

Zhenzhu Spring Group is located in the old city and mainly distributed within the area inside the enclosure of the city moat. There are 74 springs in this group, scattered in Zhenzhu Spring Yard, Baihuazhou, Furong Street, Wangfu Pond Street, Xigengdao Street, Shengfuqian Street and Daming Lake scenic spot, 10 of them belong to the "Newly Selected 72 Famous Springs", namely, Zhenzhu Spring, Sanshui Spring, Xiting Spring, Chu Spring, Zhuoying Spring, Yuhuan Spring, Furong Spring, Shun Spring, Tengjiao Spring and Shuangzhong Spring. The others are Ganyingjing Spring, Hui Spring, Zhiyu Spring, Liushi Spring, Zhusha Spring, Bukui Spring, Xiaogan Spring, Taiji Spring, Yunlou Spring, Shanmian Spring, Guangfu Spring, Xiaowangfu Pond, Qifeng Spring, Beifurong Spring, Ping Spring and several unnamed ones. These springs merge into brooks, flow into Zhuoying Lake and Baihuazhou, and finally drain into Daming Lake.

珍珠泉泉群

珍珠泉泉群地处济南老城区，大致分布在护城河以内的地区。珍珠泉泉群共有泉眼74处，相对集中于两个片区：一是珍珠泉大院内，二是附近的曲水亭、百花洲、芙蓉街、王府池子街、西更道街、省府前街及大明湖景区一带。名列"新七十二名泉"的有珍珠泉、散水泉、溪亭泉、滤泉、濯缨泉（王府池子）、玉环泉、芙蓉泉、舜泉、腾蛟泉、双忠泉等10处。其他还有感应井泉、灰泉、知鱼泉、刘氏泉、朱砂泉、不匮泉、孝感泉、太极泉、云楼泉、扇面泉、广福泉、小王府池子、起凤泉、北芙蓉泉、平泉及数处无名泉等。诸泉汇流成溪，注入濯缨湖和百花洲，最后汇入大明湖。

Zhenzhu Spring

The water bubbles out of the bottom of the pool intermittently, like bunches of pearls under sunlight. That's why it is called Zhenzhu (pearls). It is located in the yard of Standing Committee of Shandong Provincial People's Congress (No.1 Yuanqian Street, Lixia District), and to the west of the Governor's Hall in the Qing Dynasty.

珍珠泉

珍珠泉泉水自池底沙际涌出，忽聚忽散，忽断忽续，日光映之，大者如珠，小者如玑，故而得名珍珠泉。此泉位于历下区院前街1号山东省人大常委会院内，清巡抚院署大堂西。

一泓清浅漾珠圆，
细浪潆洄小荇牵。
偶与诸臣闲倚槛，
堪同渔藻入诗篇。

〔清〕爱新觉罗·玄烨《珍珠泉》

Jinan:
A City Enriched by
Famous Springs

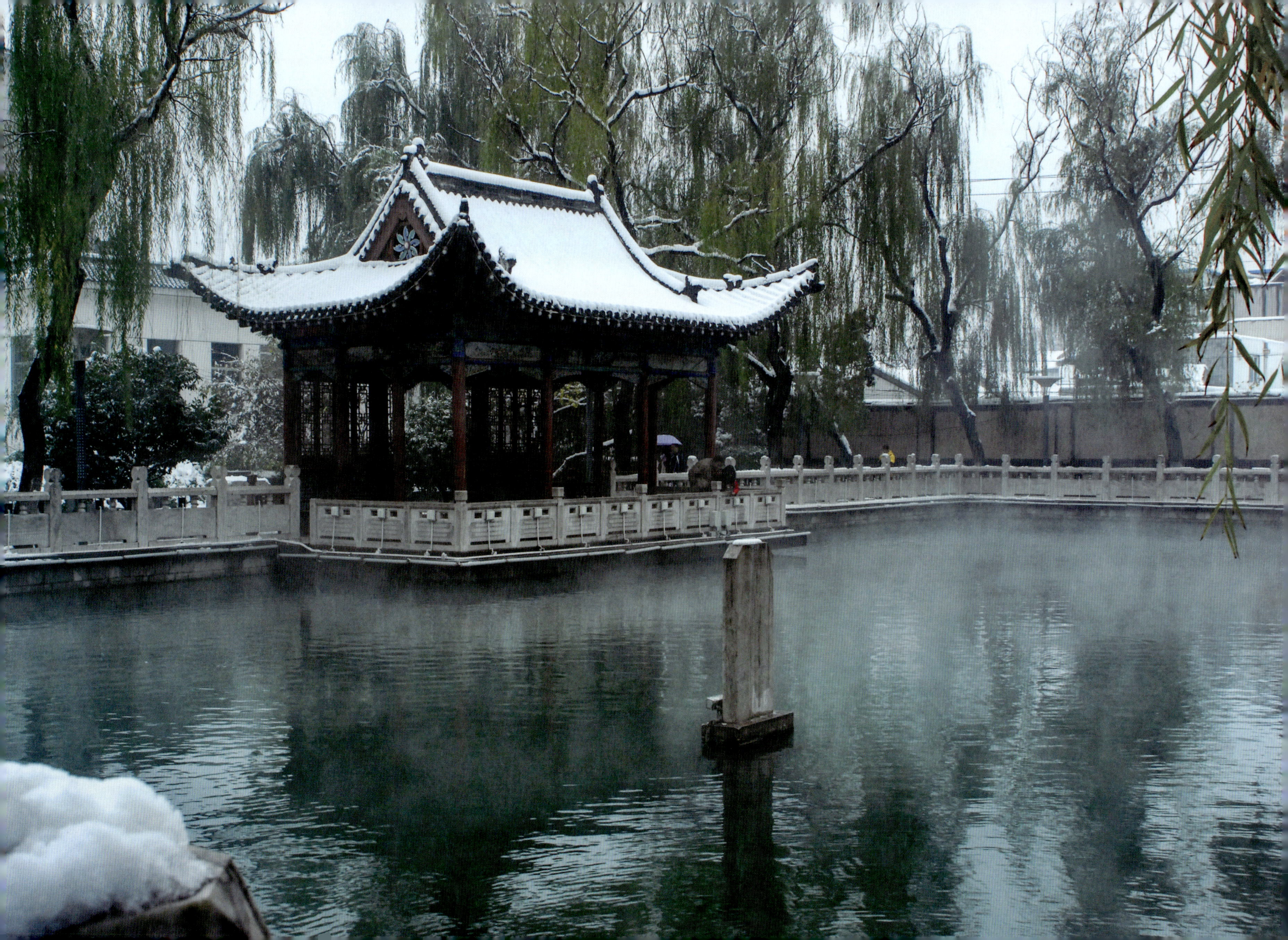

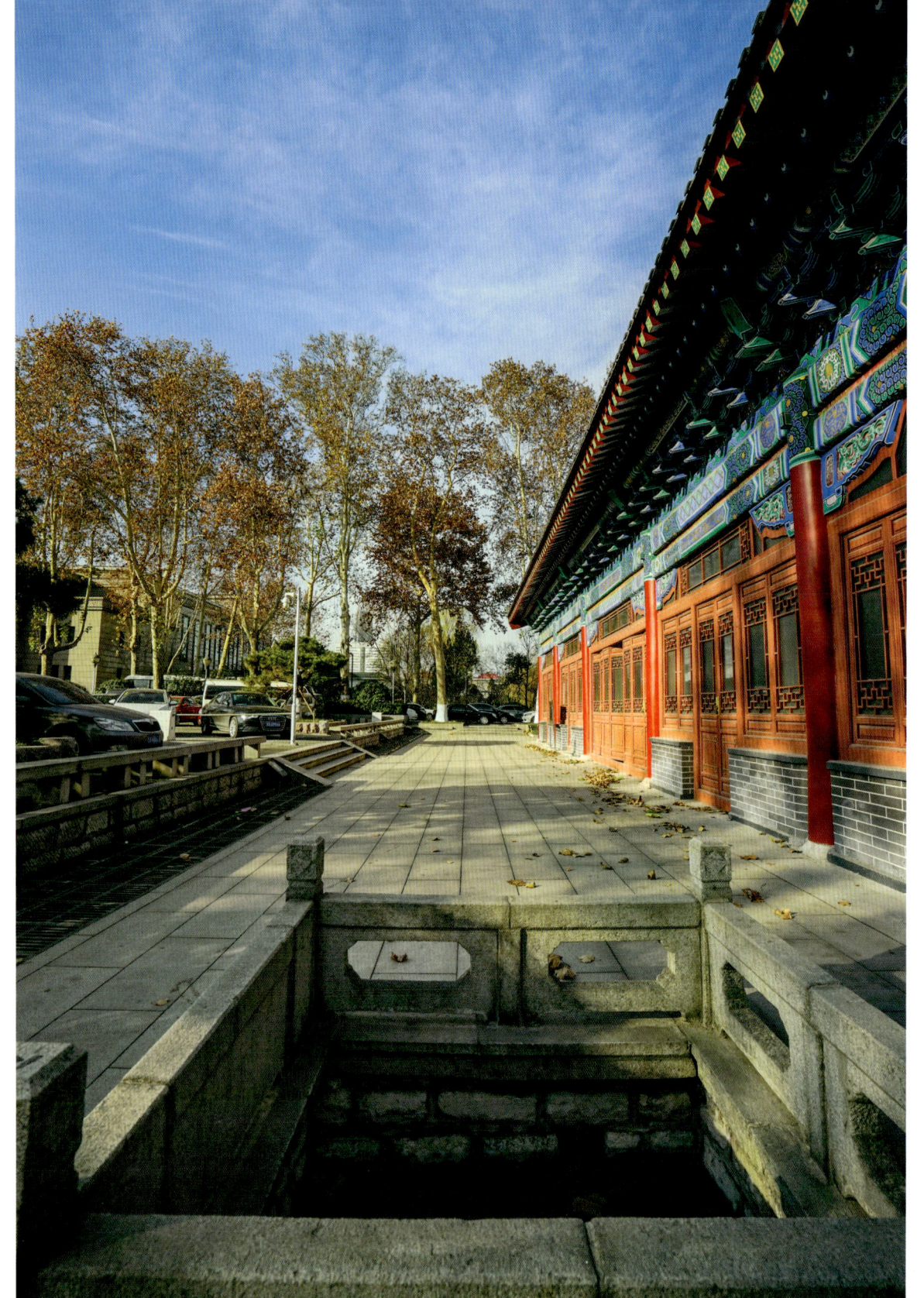

散水泉

昔日该泉的水势旺盛，泉水汩汩奋涌，水流回旋，涟漪荡漾，去而复还，聚而复散，水色空明，人们依照其水流形态名之曰"散水泉"。此泉紧邻清朝巡抚院署大堂"承运殿"，位于珍珠泉宾馆的西向。

Sanshui Spring

The abundant water spews and swirls, gets together and disperses, and flows back and forth. The water is abundant and clear. People named it for the movement of its water. It is close to the Governor's Hall in the Qing Dynasty and to the west of Zhenzhu Spring Hotel.

珠泉东向水潆洄，
荡漾涟漪去复来。
时有濯缨佳客至，
方池如鉴绝纤埃。

（明）晏璧《济南七十二泉诗》

43

Xiting Spring

There is a brook and a pavilion beside the spring. According to poetess Li Qingzhao's famous verse "Always remember the brook and pavilion under the sunset", the spring was named Xiting (brook and pavilion, also named Wangshi Xiting Spring). It is located in the yard of Standing Committee of Shandong Provincial People's Congress (No.1 Yuanqian Street, Lixia District), to the west of the Governor's Hall in the Qing Dynasty and to the east of Zhenzhu Spring.

溪亭泉

由于此泉周边溪流淙淙，亭阁翼然，遂根据宋代女词人李清照的"常记溪亭日暮"诗句中"溪亭"一词为之命名，又名"王氏溪亭泉"。此泉位于历下区院前街1号院内，清巡抚院署大堂西，珍珠泉东。

鱼池西北水涓涓，
王氏溪亭尚翼然。
溪上槐阴清昼永，
凭栏徙倚听鸣蝉。
（明）晏璧《济南七十二泉诗》

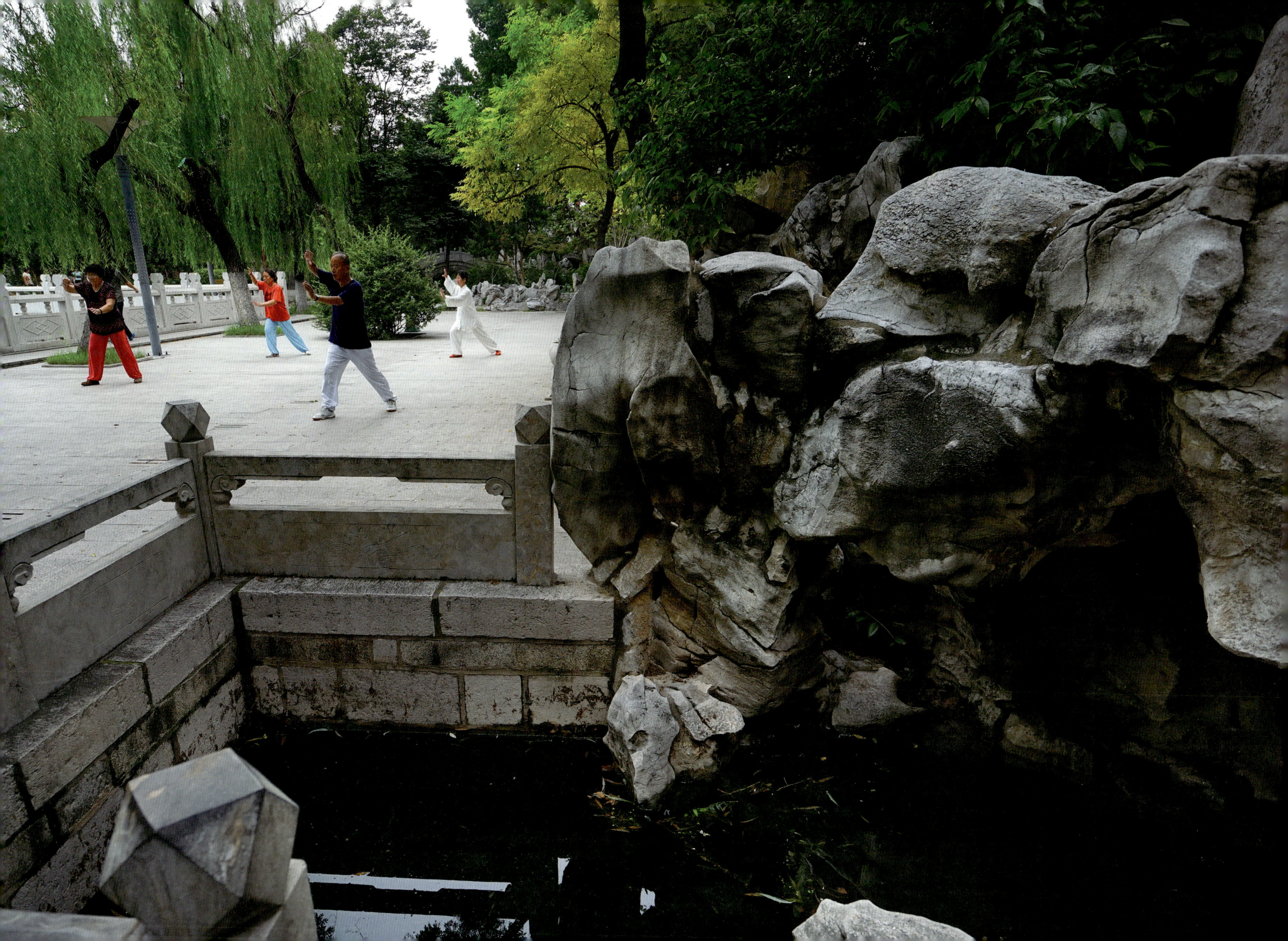

濯缨泉，取《孟子》"清斯濯缨，浊斯濯足"之意而命名。由于该泉泉池阔大，又称"濯缨湖"。旧时，该泉位于德王府内，故当地百姓称其为"王府池子"。该泉泉水味甘清冽，水草摇曳；池岸民居错落，曲径通幽，杨柳叠翠，水流成溪，是人们领略济南老城风情的极佳去处。该泉位于历下区王府池子街中段。

Zhuoying Spring (Wangfu Pond)

Zhuo means "wash"; ying means "the belt on the hat". Zhuoying Spring is derived from "Clean water can be used to wash the belt on the hat; cloudy water can be used to wash one's feet" in *Mencius*. Since the spring is really big, it is also called Zhuoying Lake. The spring is located in the Palace of Prince De, so the local people also call it Wangfu (prince's palace) Pond. The water is sweet and cool with waterweeds growing in it. Houses are scattered around the banks. Winding paths lead to hidden spots. Willows show thick greenness. It is good place for people to appreciate the flavor of the old city of Jinan. It is located in the midpiece of Wangfu Pond Street, Lixia District.

钓艇飘然过历亭,
芦花漠漠水泠泠。
画栏四面多秋柳,
犹有渔洋几树青。

［清］刘考《雍缪湖》

晴霞飞不断,
湖水含泓澄。
一丛白菡萏,
无数红蜻蜓。
我爱许长史,
诗思何泠泠。
（清）田雯
《许殿卿书楼在芙蓉泉西》

Furong Spring

Lotus flowers were called Furong by Chinese people in ancient times. People in Jinan have been keeping a special love for the lotus flower, naming the spring with it. The street in which the spring is located also follows the name Furong. It is located in the south of a small square outside No. 69 Furong Street.

芙蓉泉

芙蓉者，荷花也。济南人自古以来就对荷花情有独钟，更是用它做了一泓泉水的名字，泉池所在的街道遂以泉名而命名"芙蓉街"。该泉位于历下区芙蓉街69号院外小广场南部。

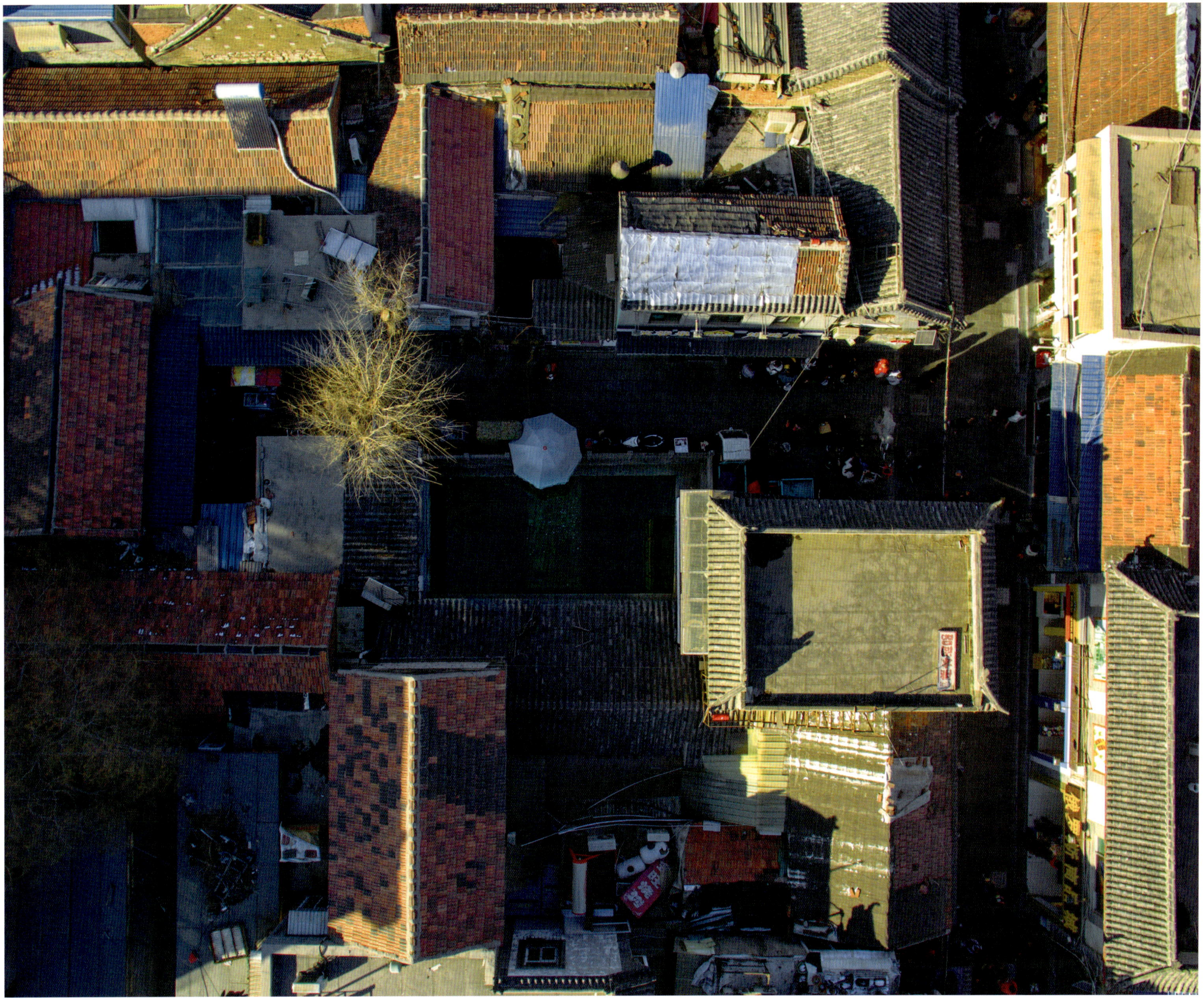

齐南郡里多沮洳，
娥皇女英汲井处。
窃向池中潜哄来，
浇茆溪上平流去。

[唐]魏炎　见《封氏闻见记》

Shun Spring

Shun Spring is also called Shun Well. It is said that it was dug out by Shun, the great tribe league leader in primitive society. Shun's wives, Ehuang and Nyuying, used to wash clothes with its water. The famous geographer, Li Daoyuan, did a comprehensive research on it in his work *Shuijing Zhu* (*Commentary on the Waterways Classic*). It is on the west side of Shunjing Road and 200m away from the crossing of Quancheng Road and Shunjing Road.

舜泉
（舜井）

舜泉又称舜井，世传是由大舜亲手凿挖而成，舜的妻子娥皇和女英每天都从这里汲水浣衣。早在1400多年前，著名地理学家郦道元在其所著《水经注》中，就对舜井做过详尽考证。此泉位于历下区泉城路与舜井街交叉口南行200米路西。

舜 井

　　古史传说，虞舜疏浚此井。北魏郦道元《水经注》记载，历城城南对山，山上有舜祠，山下有大穴，谓之舜井。舜井为大舜遗泽，历代多有著录与题咏。

Tengjiao Spring

In the past, the examination office and Confucius' Temple were in this area. There was a stone archway on which the characters "soaring dragon and rising phoenix" were engraved. It was used to encourage the students in Jinan to study hard and pursue bright future. Later, people named the two nearby springs "Tengjiao" (soaring dragon) and "Qifeng" (rising phoenix). It is on the east side of the north end of Wangfu Pond Street.

腾蛟泉

　　过去，腾蛟泉一带建有贡院、文庙等，街上有一石坊，上刻"腾蛟起凤"四个大字，以此来激励应试的学子刻苦攻读。后来，人们便把石坊附近的两处泉水，分别命名为"腾蛟泉"和"起凤泉"。腾蛟泉位于历下区王府池子街北首路东。

王府池子街
WANG FU CHI ZI JIE

2500 11

腾蛟泉

腾蛟泉碑记

里巷浅碧泓，
秋水玉镜中。
斜阳留晚照，
一夕腾蛟龙。

拾荒《腾蛟泉》

Jinan:
A City Enriched by Famous Springs

Heihu Spring Group

泉群 黑虎泉

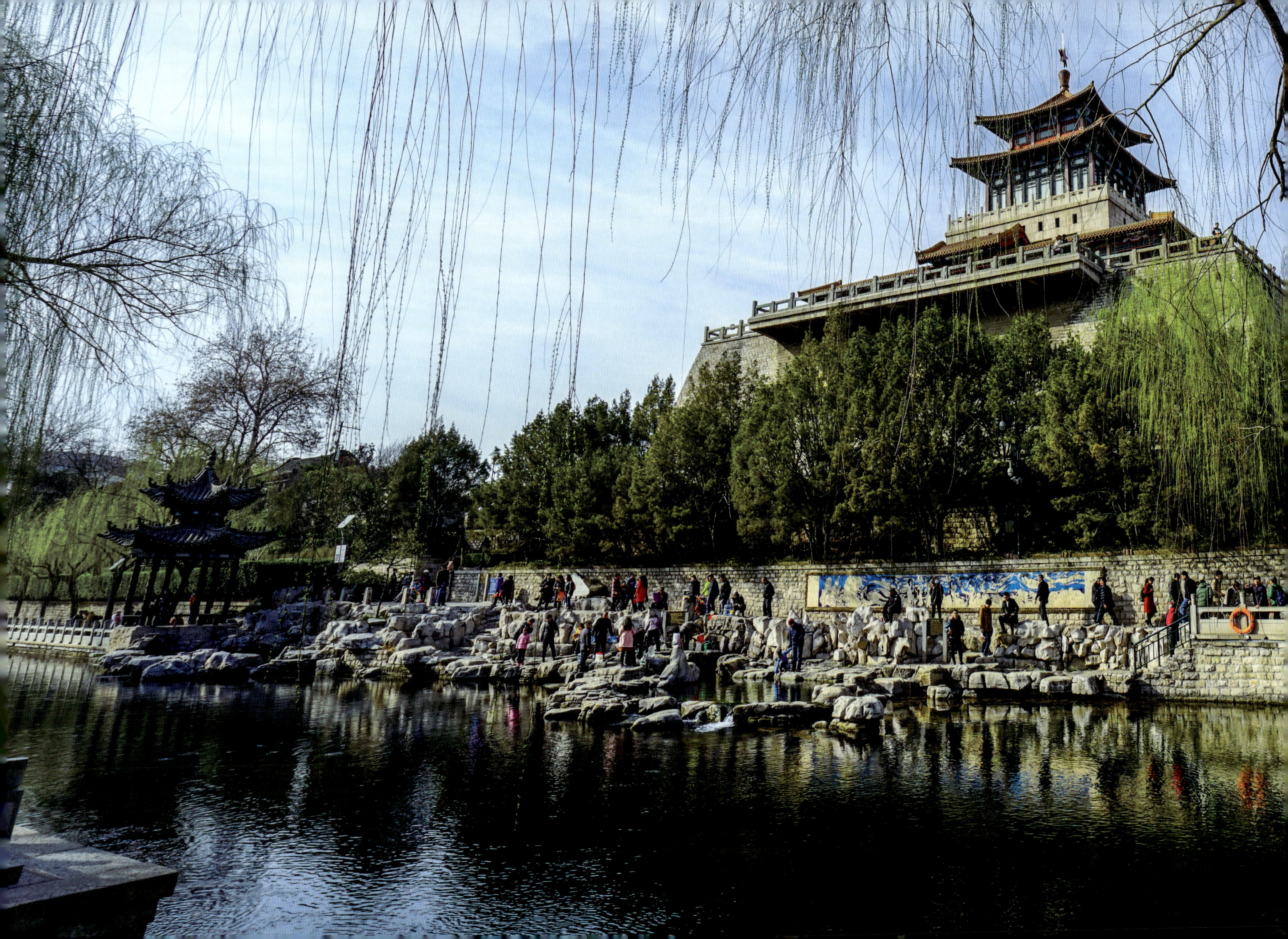

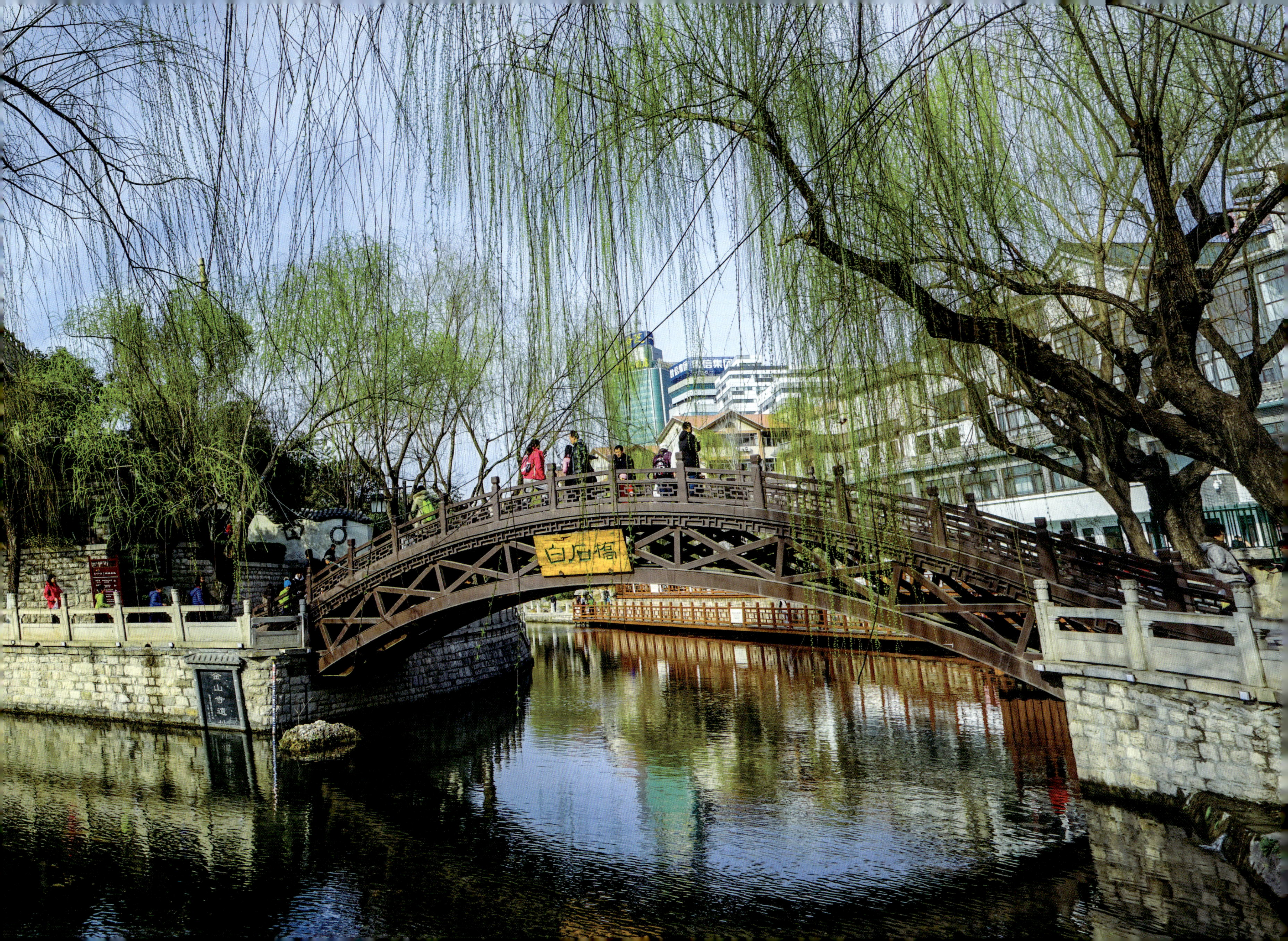

Heihu Spring Group

Heihu Spring Group is in the southeast of the old city of Jinan. There are 16 springs distributed on the banks of the south moat or in the river. Heihu Spring, Pipa Spring, Manao Spring, Baishi Spring and Jiunyu Spring are among the "Newly Selected 72 Famous Springs". The other springs are Jinhu Spring, Nanzhenzhu Spring, Douya Spring, Wulian Spring, Ren Spring, Yinsi Spring, Huibo Spring, Duibo Spring, Yihu Spring (also called Miaojia Spring), Gujian Spring, and Shoukang Spring.

黑虎泉泉群

黑虎泉泉群位于济南老城东南隅，沿南护城河岸分布，共有泉池16处。其中，黑虎泉、琵琶泉、玛瑙泉、白石泉、九女泉5处属于"新七十二名泉"之列。其他泉还有金虎泉、南珍珠泉、豆芽泉、五莲泉、任泉、胤嗣泉、汇波泉、对波泉、一虎泉（一称缪家泉）、古鉴泉和寿康泉。

Heihu Spring

The water beats the rocks, which sounds like roar of tigers, so the spring was named Heihu (black tiger). There used to be a Water God Temple called Heihu Temple on the upper bank. The water spews out of the mouths of three stone beasts in a massive manner, and pours into the pool like three hanging curtains. The sprays are of different shapes, some are like snow, and some are like fog. It is on the south bank of the east end of the south moat, and can be overlooked from the upstairs of Jinan Liberation Pavilion.

黑虎泉

黑虎泉因其"水击巨石,声如虎啸"而得名。原泉上崖畔建有水神庙,称黑虎庙。该泉水势浩大,澄澈可鉴须眉,巨流从三个兽口中喷薄而出,澎湃万状,飘者若雪,断者若雾,缀者如旒,挂者如帘。泉池位于南护城河东首南岸,登解放阁俯瞰西南可见。

Jinan:
A City Enriched by
Famous Springs

悬崖之下碧潭深，
潭上悬崖欲几寻。
石激湍声成虎吼，
泉喷清响作龙吟。
寒光一声常惊骨，
澄色千年可洗心。
最喜酒家多野趣，
相携同醉绿杨荫。
〔明〕刘敕《咏黑虎泉》

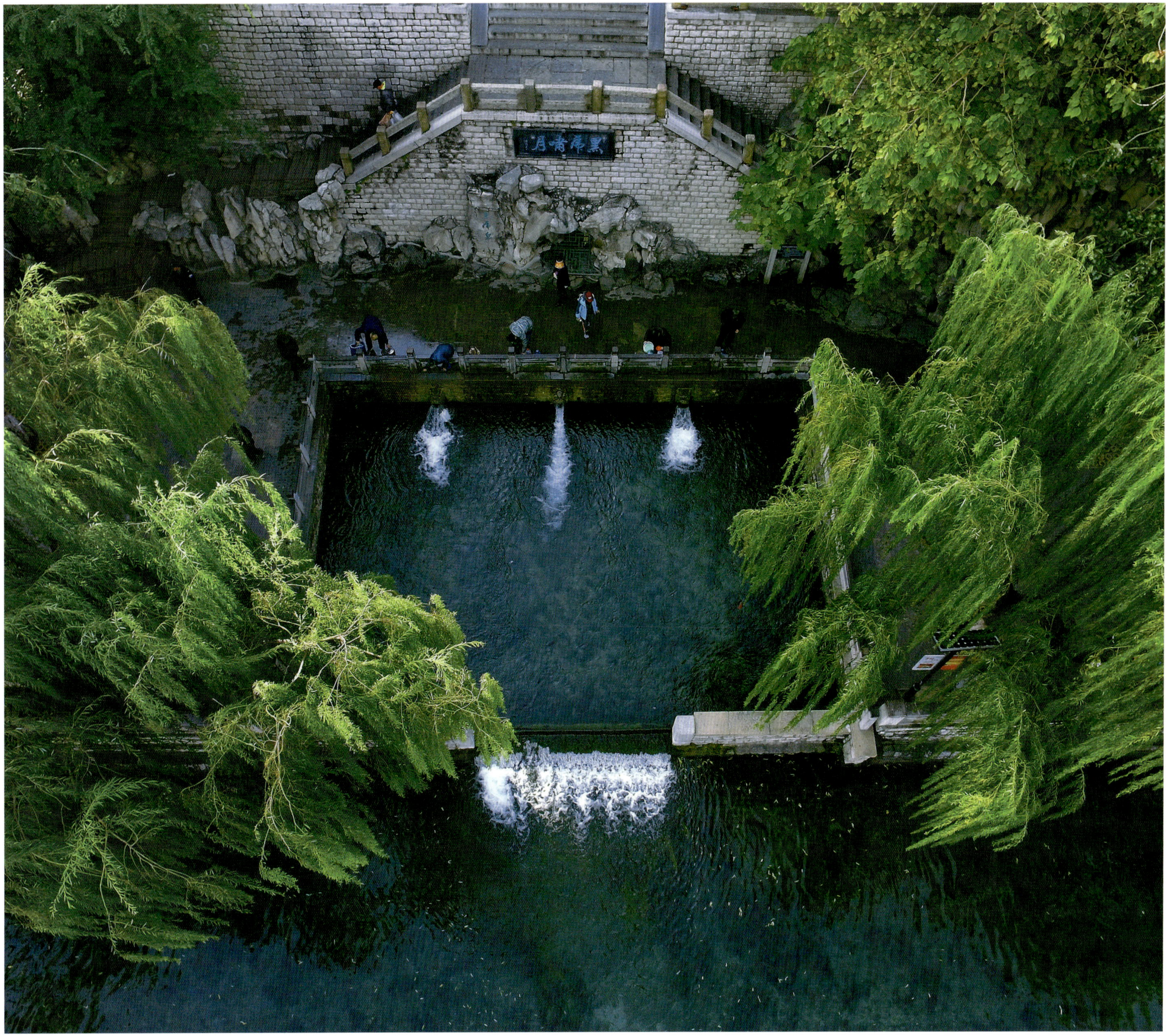

大弦嘈嘈如急雨,
小弦切切如私语。
嘈嘈切切错杂弹,
大珠小珠落玉盘。
〔唐〕白居易《琵琶行》节选

琵琶泉

琵琶泉因水声淙淙,犹若琵琶奏鸣之声而得名。泉水由池底涌出,漫溢二级台阶,跌宕而下,落入护城河中,状若琴弦,与河水相击,声如琴音。该泉位于南护城河南岸,黑虎泉西,五莲泉东,琵琶桥下。

Pipa Spring

The spring water gurgles, reminding people of the sound of Pipa (a Chinese musical instrument). The water spews from the bottom of the pool, overflows the second step, and falls into the moat. The falling streams look like strings and sound like the Pipa. It is on the south bank of the south moat, to the west of Heihu Spring, to the east of Wulian Spring and under the Pipa Bridge.

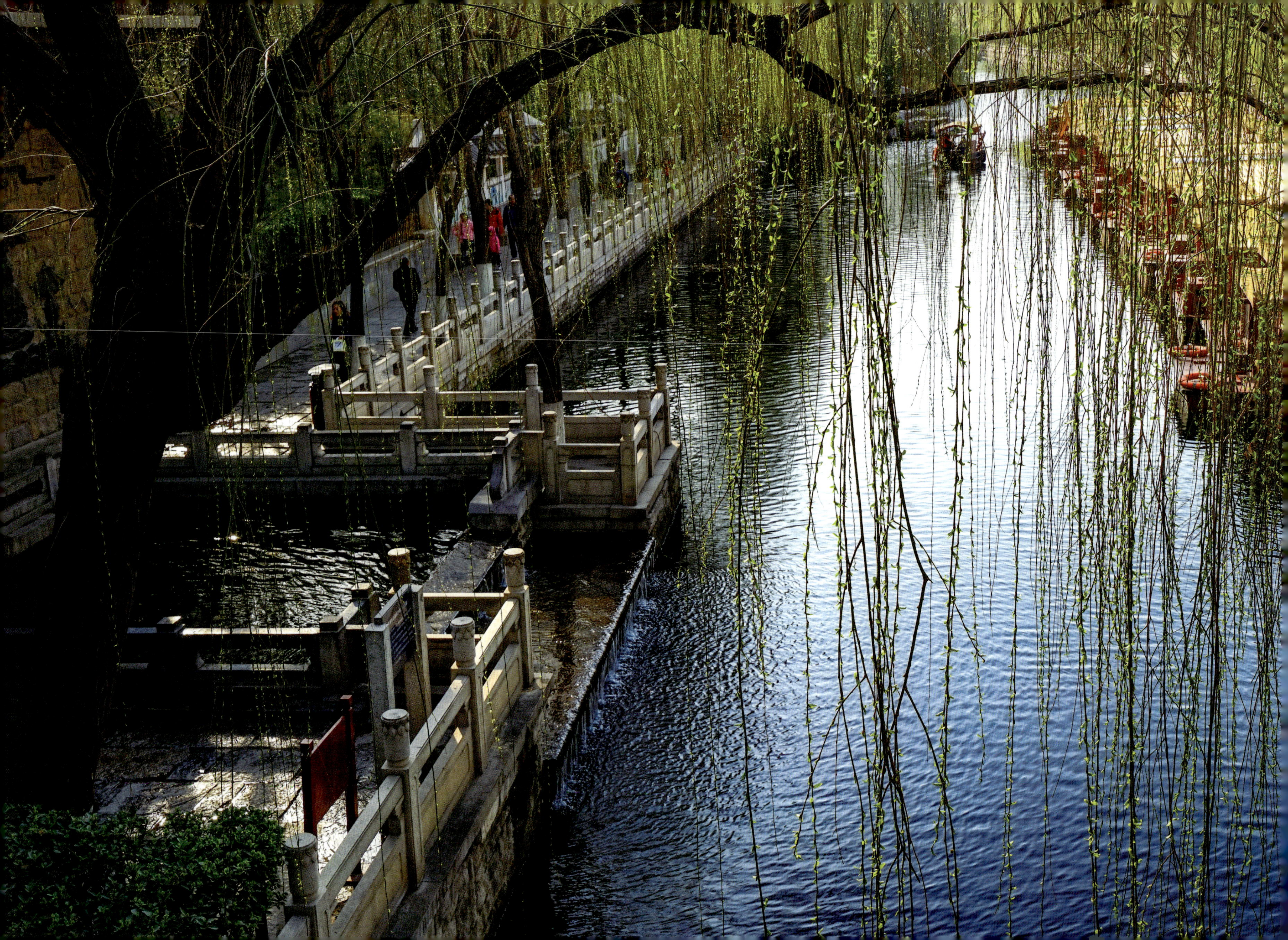

燕舞莺歌三月天，
风拂柳条玛瑙喧。
泠泠奏曲藏虹气，
一泉荡曳翠满园。

拾荒《咏玛瑙泉》

玛瑙泉

玛瑙泉因水自池底涌起串串水泡，经阳光照射，五彩缤纷，犹如玛瑙一般而得名。该泉冬夏两季盛水期，水势洪大，水色碧绿。泉水溢满后，从北池壁高于护城河河水的6个方形洞孔中泄入河中。此泉位于南护城河东首南岸，北对白石泉，仰望解放阁。

Manao Spring

The water bubbles, rising up from the bottom of the pool, are colorful under the sunlight, just like agates. That's why people call the spring "Manao"(agate). The water is so clear that you can see the bottom. The water is most abundant in winter and summer, overflows into the moat from six square holes on the north wall of the pool. It is on the south bank of the east end of the south moat, opposite Baishi Spring and below Jinan Liberation Pavilion.

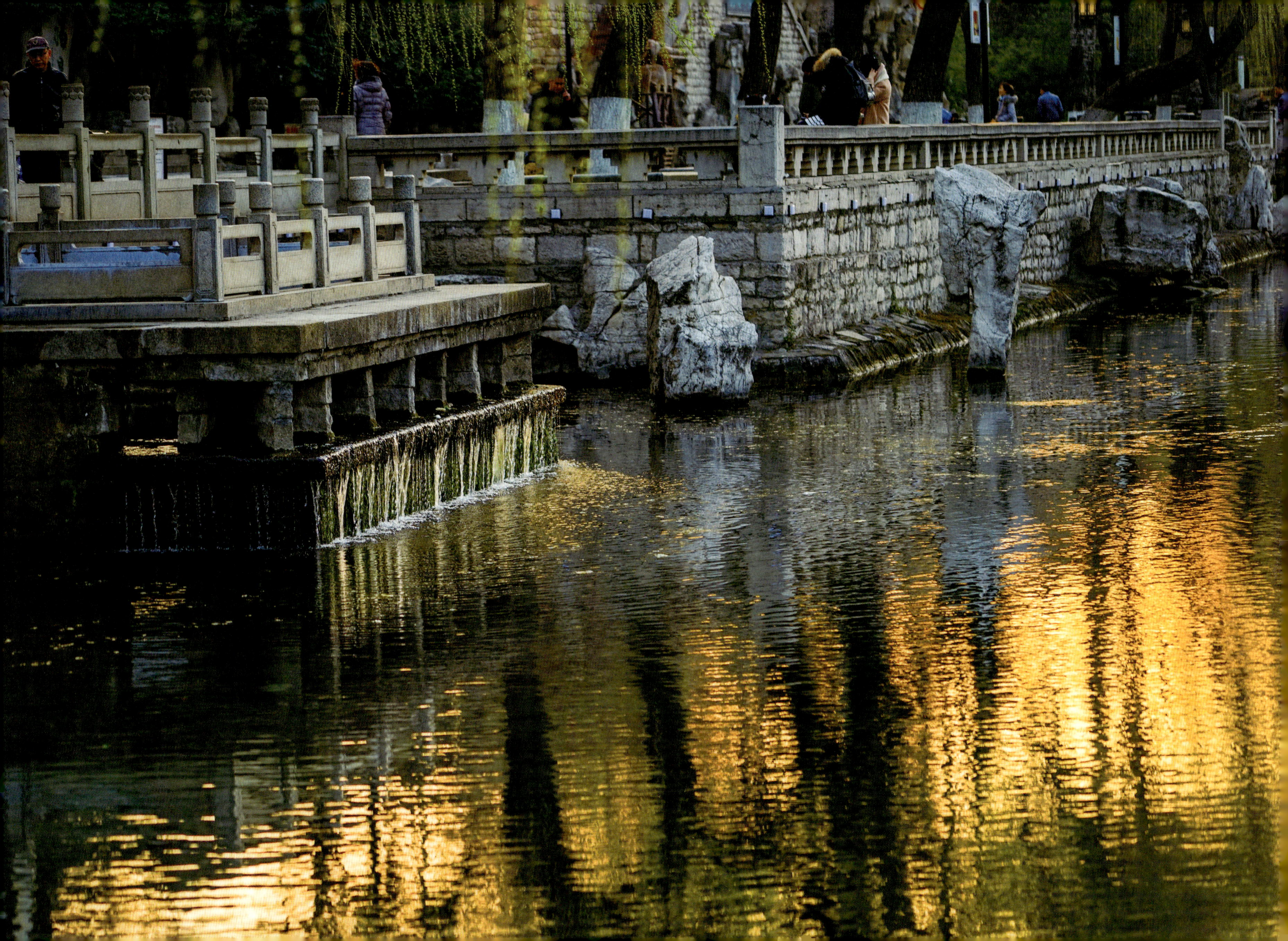

白石泉

1794年春末，时值济南大旱，时任山东布政使的江兰主持疏浚护城河工程。河工挖掘河道时，忽有泉水涌出，味甘如醴，既能灌溉农田，又能汲取饮用，因泉周有粼粼白石出没于水面，人们便将它命名为"白石泉"。该泉位于南护城河东首北岸，登解放阁南侧可俯瞰其全貌。

Baishi Spring

In the late spring of 1794, a drought hit Jinan. The Shandong Governor Jiang Lan organized a project of dredging the moat. When the laborers were digging the river course, a spring spewed out. Around the spring, sparkling white stones emerged over the surface of water. The water is extremely sweet, and can be used both for irrigation and drinking. Therefore, the spring is called Baishi (white stone). It is on the north bank of the east end of the south moat, and can be overlooked from the upstairs of Jinan Liberation Pavilion.

料峭西风雁一行，无聊情味是秋光。
断桥聚影没残碣，远水跳波喧夕阳。
杯泛碧螺清酒吻，花开红蓼媚茶铛。
碑文去读金山寺，齿冷何人笑欲狂。

（清）陈超《白石泉茶肆即事》

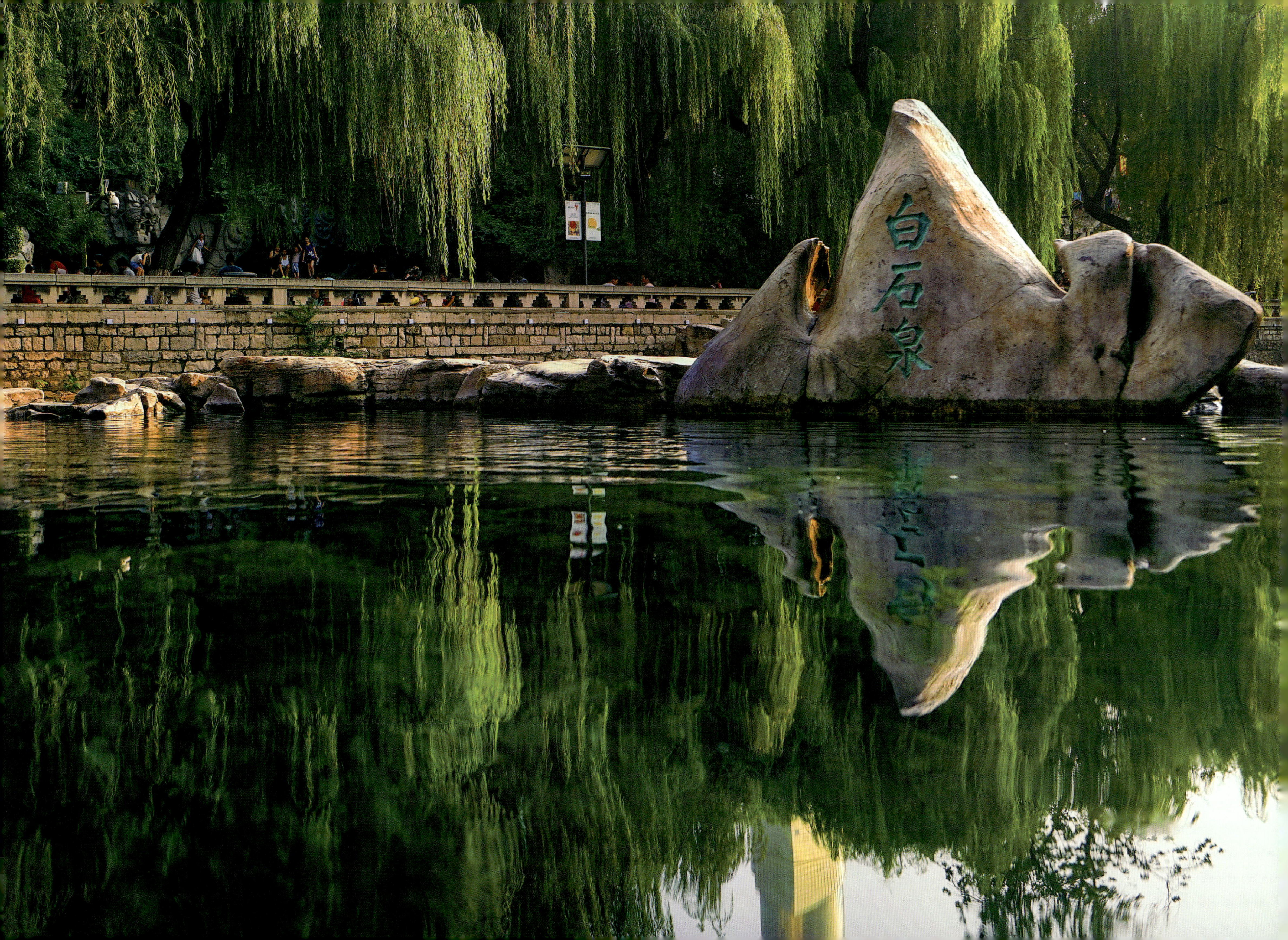
白石泉

Jiunyu Spring

In the past, there was a Kuixing Pavilion built on the southeast corner of the old city wall. It was on the north of the spring. It was said that the pavilion was transformed from fairy maidens. Therefore, the pavilion was also called Jiunyu Pavilion, and the spring under the pavilion was named likewise. According to a folk story, nine white-dressed fairies came to bathe in the spring every night and left in the second morning. It is below the southwest corner of Jinan Liberation Pavilion, on the north bank of the south moat and to the west of Baishi Spring.

九女泉

旧时，该泉北侧是济南古城墙，城墙东南角建有魁星阁一座。相传魁星是由九天仙女变化而来，因此魁星阁又被称为"九女楼"，楼下的这处泉水自然被称为"九女泉"了。据传，每到夜晚会有九位白衣仙女来此沐浴，天明即飘然而去。此泉位于解放阁西南角，南护城河北岸，白石泉西邻。

石瓮方塘滃然出，迸散不息化珍珠。
荇藻离披冬犹绿，九天仙女倚树竹。
——拾荒《九女泉》

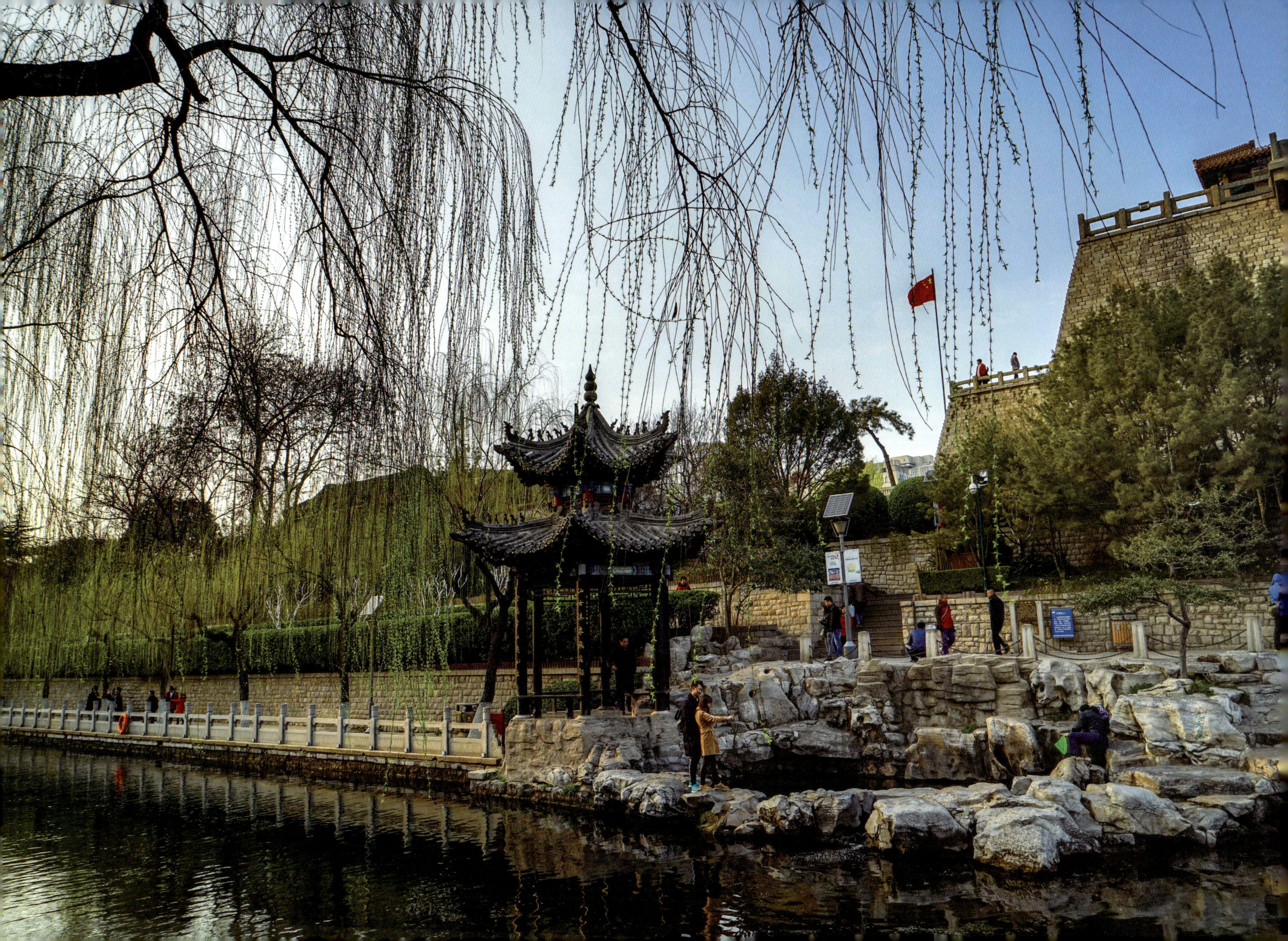

Jinan:
A City Enriched by Famous Springs

Wulong Pond Spring Group

五龙潭
泉群

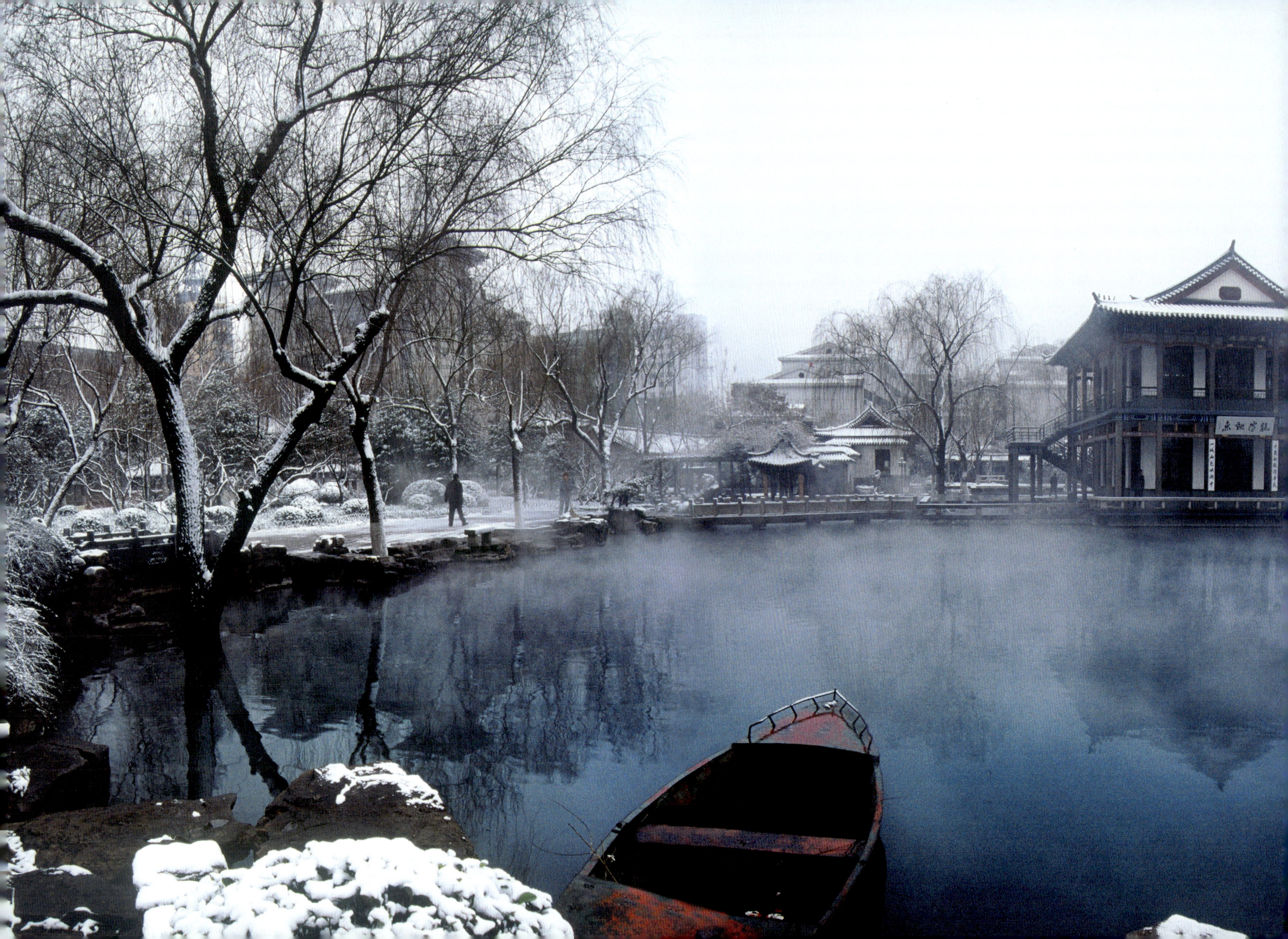

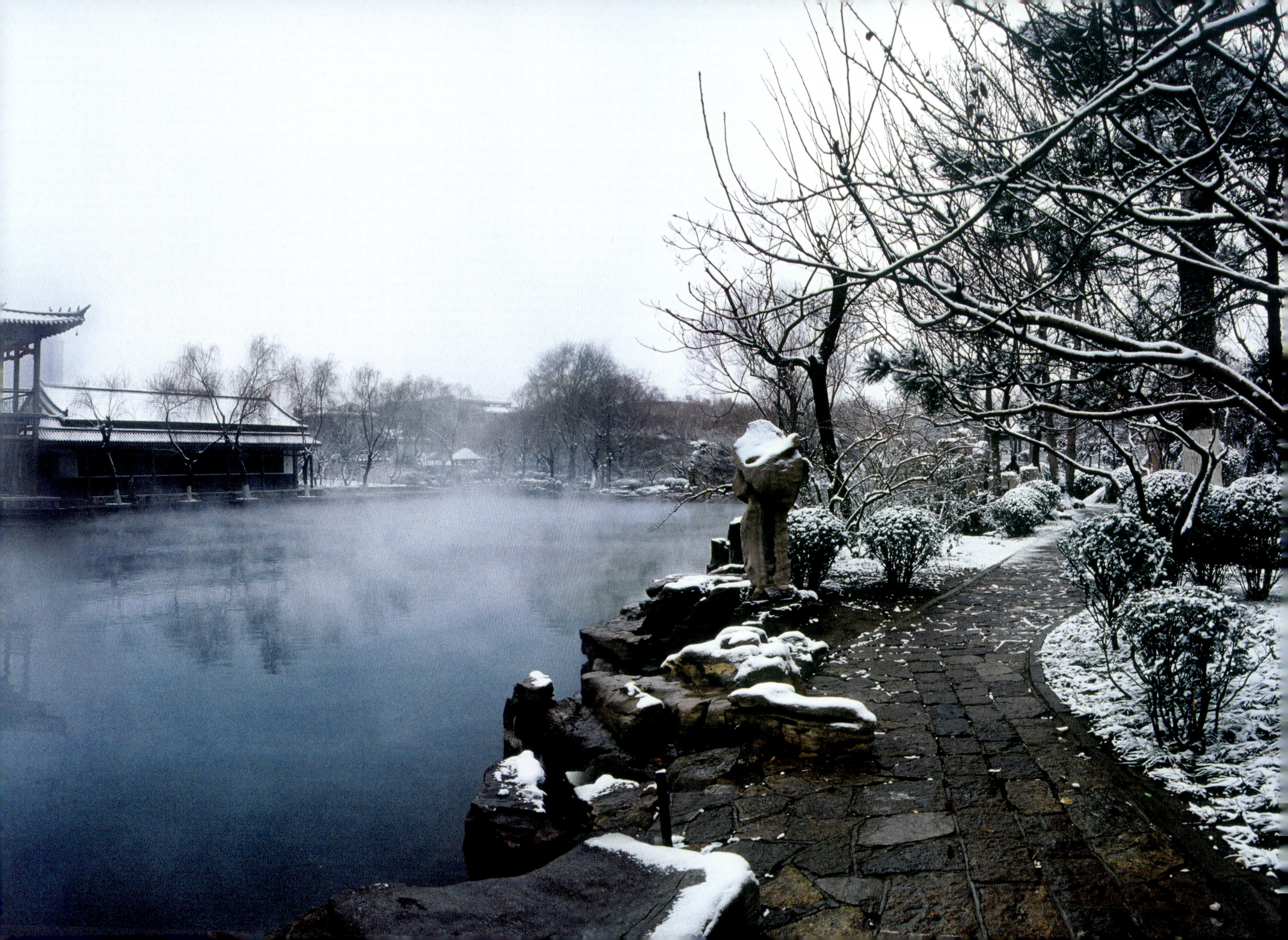

Wulong Pond Spring Group

Most of the 28 springs are in Wulong Pond Park. Wulong Pond, Guwen Spring, Xianqing Spring, Tianjing Spring, Yueya Spring, Ximizhi Spring, Guanjia Pond, Huima Spring, Qiuxi Spring, Yu Spring, and Lian Spring are among the "Newly Selected 72 Famous Springs". The others are Dongmizhi Spring, Xixin Spring, Jingshui Spring, Jingchi Spring, Dongliu Spring, Beixibo Spring, Lexi Spring, Tanxi Spring, Qishisan Spring, Qing Spring, Jing Spring, Jingming Spring, Xianming Spring, Yuhong Spring, Conger Spring, Chi Spring and Li Spring etc.

五龙潭泉群

五龙潭泉群大部分泉址在今五龙潭公园内，共有泉28处，其中，五龙潭、古温泉、贤清泉、天镜泉、月牙泉、西蜜脂泉、官家池、回马泉、虬溪泉、玉泉、濂泉计11处属于"新七十二名泉"之列。其他泉还有东蜜脂泉、洗心泉、静水泉、净池泉、东流泉、北洗钵泉、泺溪泉、潭西泉、七十三泉、青泉、井泉、睛明泉、显明池、裕宏泉、聪耳泉、赤泉、醴泉等。

Wulong Pond

It was called Jing Pond in the past. There is a pavilion beside the pond, which was built in the Tang Dynasty, namely, Lixia Pavilion. In 745, a famous poet Du Fu came here attending a feast and wrote: "This pavilion in Shandong has a long history, and the city of Jinan has a long list of celebrities." At that time, Wulong Pond was a part of Daming Lake. Later, a small temple was built beside the pond and there were five statues for worshiping. Therefore, the pond is called Wulong (five dragons). It is in Wulong Pond Park, which is to the north of Ximen Bridge.

五龙潭

　　五龙潭，古时称为"净池"，池边建有客亭一座，即唐代的历下亭。唐天宝四年（745），诗人杜甫在此即席写下"海右此亭古，济南名士多"的佳句。彼时，五龙潭为古大明湖的一部分。后来有人在潭边修建小庙一座，塑五神像供奉，于是便有了"五龙潭"的名称。此潭位于西门桥以北的五龙潭公园内。

传是蛟龙宅,
龙潜何处寻?
坛中台殿古,
门外石潭深。
树密云常合,
亭高日半阴。
坐来水色净,
聊可空人心。

〔明〕刘敩《五龙潭》

Jinan:
A City Enriched by Famous Springs

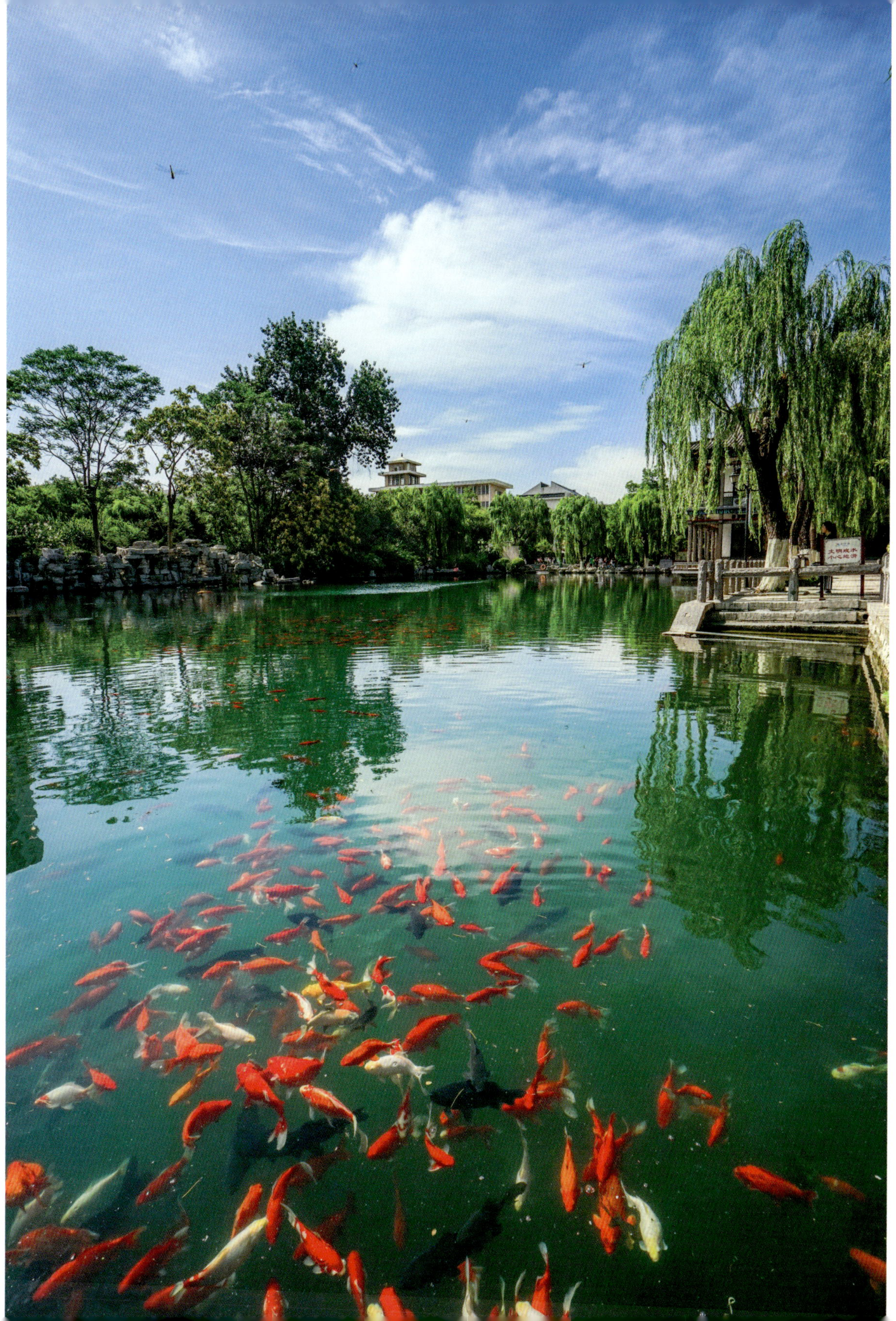

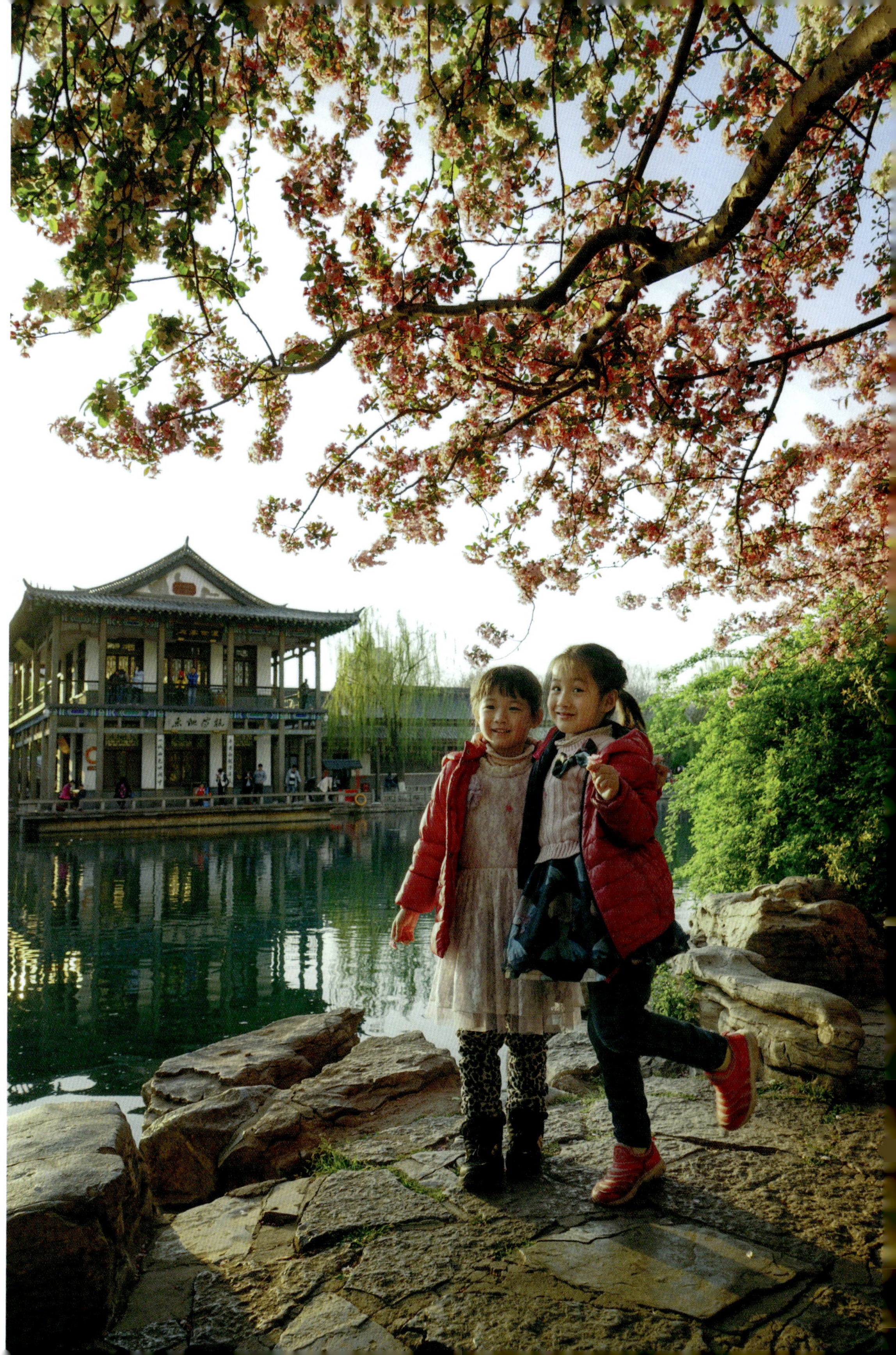

太真偏爱浴华清，
温润何如历下城。
玉韫昆山何借润，
不劳薪楛与煎烹。

〔明〕晏璧《济南七十二泉诗》

古温泉

此泉泉水常年恒温，在18℃左右，尤其到了隆冬时节，天寒地冻、朔风刺骨，泉池内却是热气蒸腾、云烟缭绕，故得名"温泉"，后因其历史久远，人们习惯上称之为"古温泉"。该泉位于五龙潭公园南部。

Guwen Spring

The water keeps a steady temperature at about 18℃. In winter, it is chilly and windy everywhere, but the spring is hovered by warm steam and fog. In addition, the spring has a long history, so it is called Guwen (old and warm). It is in the southern part of Wulong Pond Park.

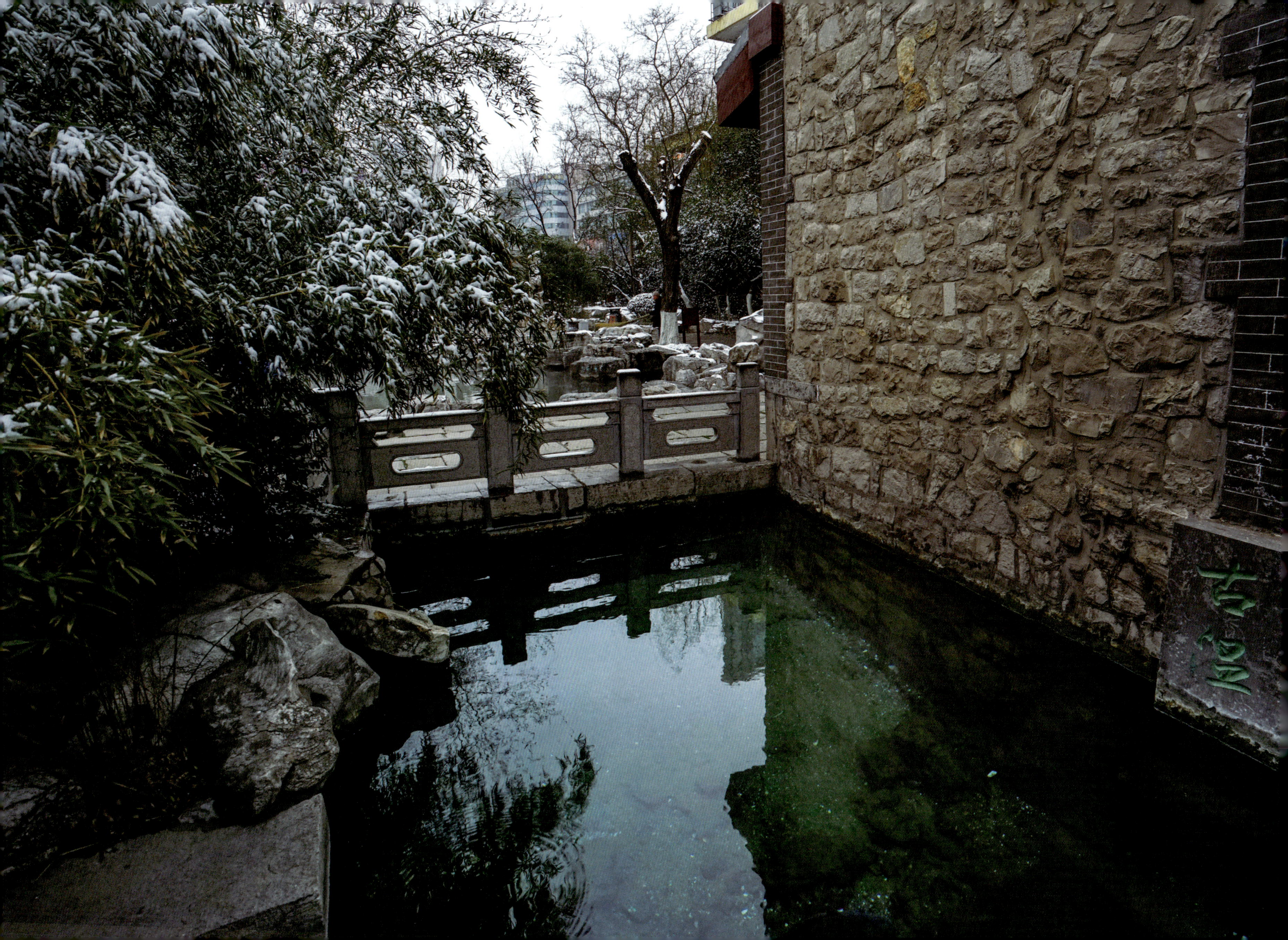
古温

Xianqing Spring

It was called Xuanqing Spring in the past and was given the present name in the Ming Dynasty. The water is clear and sweet, and good for making tea. In old days, scholars often gathered here, fishing, drinking, and exchanging ideas. It is also a good place for people to summer. It is in the northeast corner of Wulong Spring Park.

贤清泉

风竹杂泉声,斜阳林外横。偶来池上酌,坐待晚凉生。萤拂花光乱,蝉鸣露气清。举杯见明月,流影过高城。

〔清〕张仞《贤清园杂咏四首》其一

　　贤清泉,古时也称"悬清泉",是一处消暑的胜地。其泉水清冽甘美,最适合煮酒泡茶。过去,文人雅士常在此处月下听泉,阶上垂钓,酌酒品茗,怀古论今。该泉位于五龙潭公园东北隅。

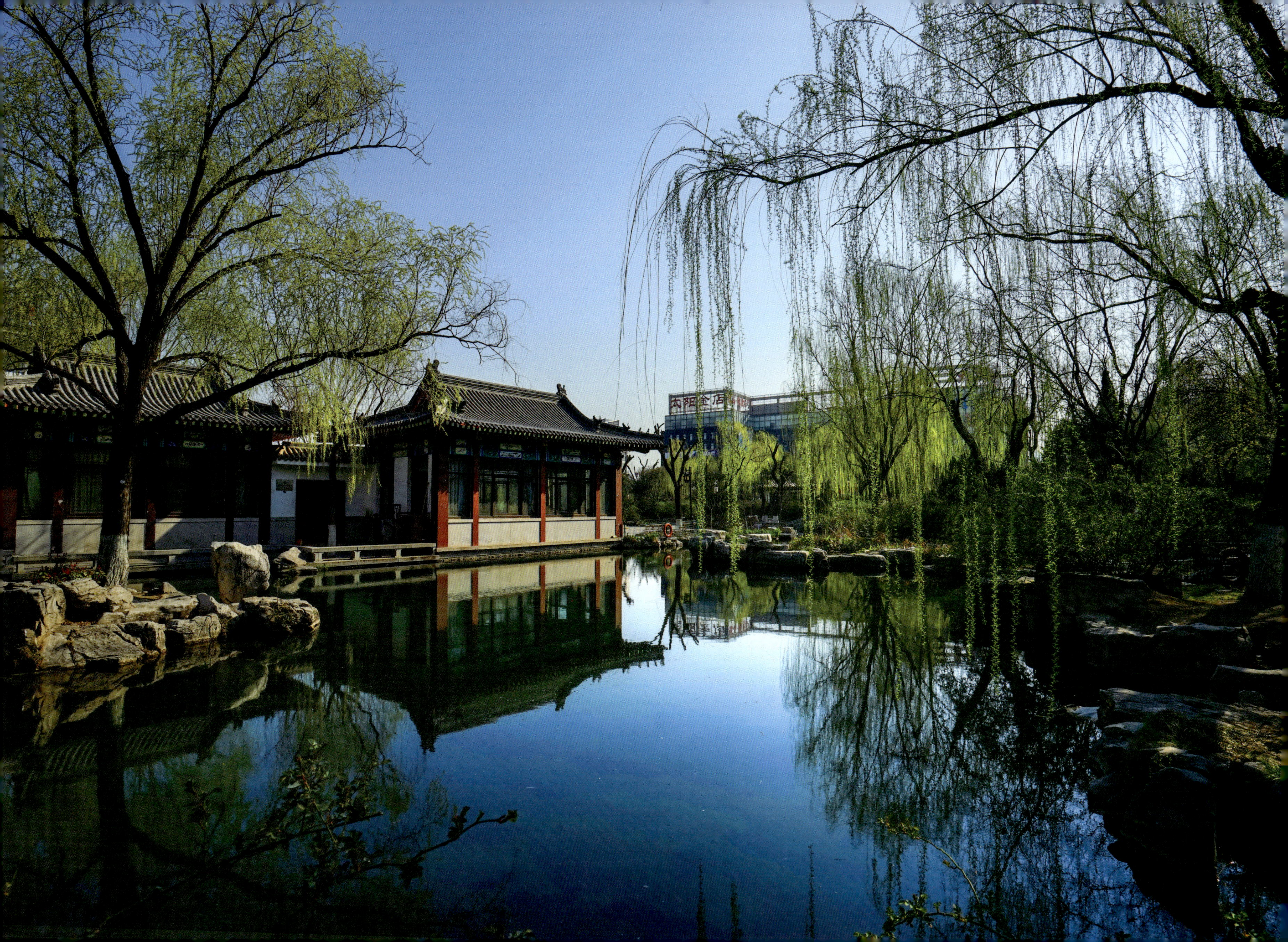
太阳金店

Tianjing Spring

The spring is so flat and clean that it looks like the real sky with the reflections of the sun, the moon and the stars in it. Therefore, it was named Tianjing (sky mirror). In the Ming Dynasty, a military officer whose family name was Jiang lived beside the spring. Therefore, it is also called Jiangjia Pond. When the water is abundant, strings of bubbles rise up from the sands to the surface and pop, creating exquisite ripples. It is in the northeast corner of Wulong Spring Park, and to the west of the south gate of the park.

天镜泉（江家池）

因泉水平明，日月星辰倒影犹如高天垂镜，因而得名"天镜泉"。明代嘉靖年间，有江姓武官世居于此，故又被称为"江家池"。盛水期时，泉水自沙际冒出，成串水泡升至水面破裂，形成一道道美丽的花纹。该泉位于五龙潭公园东北隅，公园南门西侧。

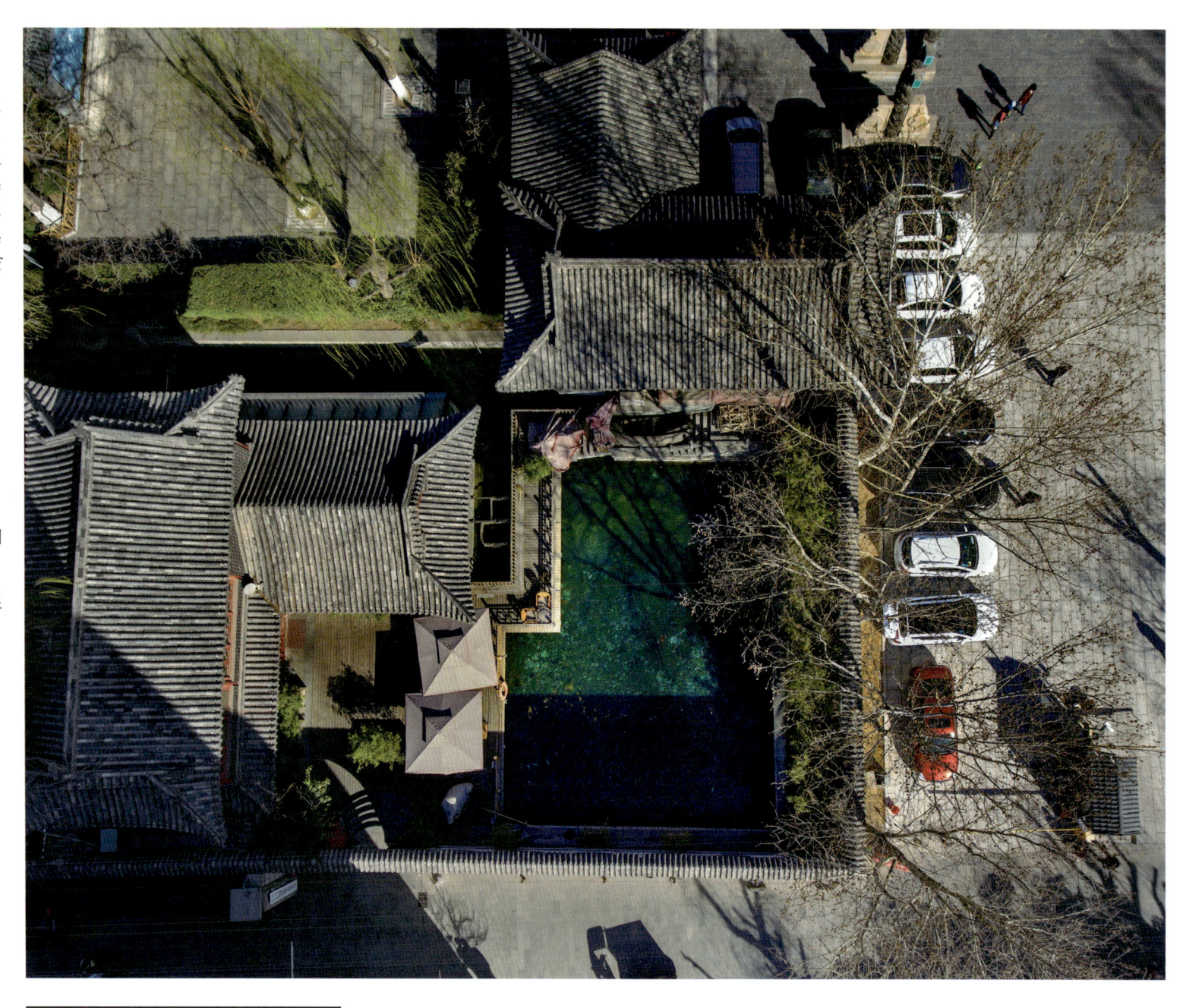

> 一方明镜自天来，嵌入院前台。
> 映碧落浮白，时青蔚、云纱复开。
> 光滑玉润，晶莹剔透，水下隐苍苔。
> 藻草触鱼鳃，雨过后、蛙声难衰。
>
> 王化学《太常引·天镜泉》

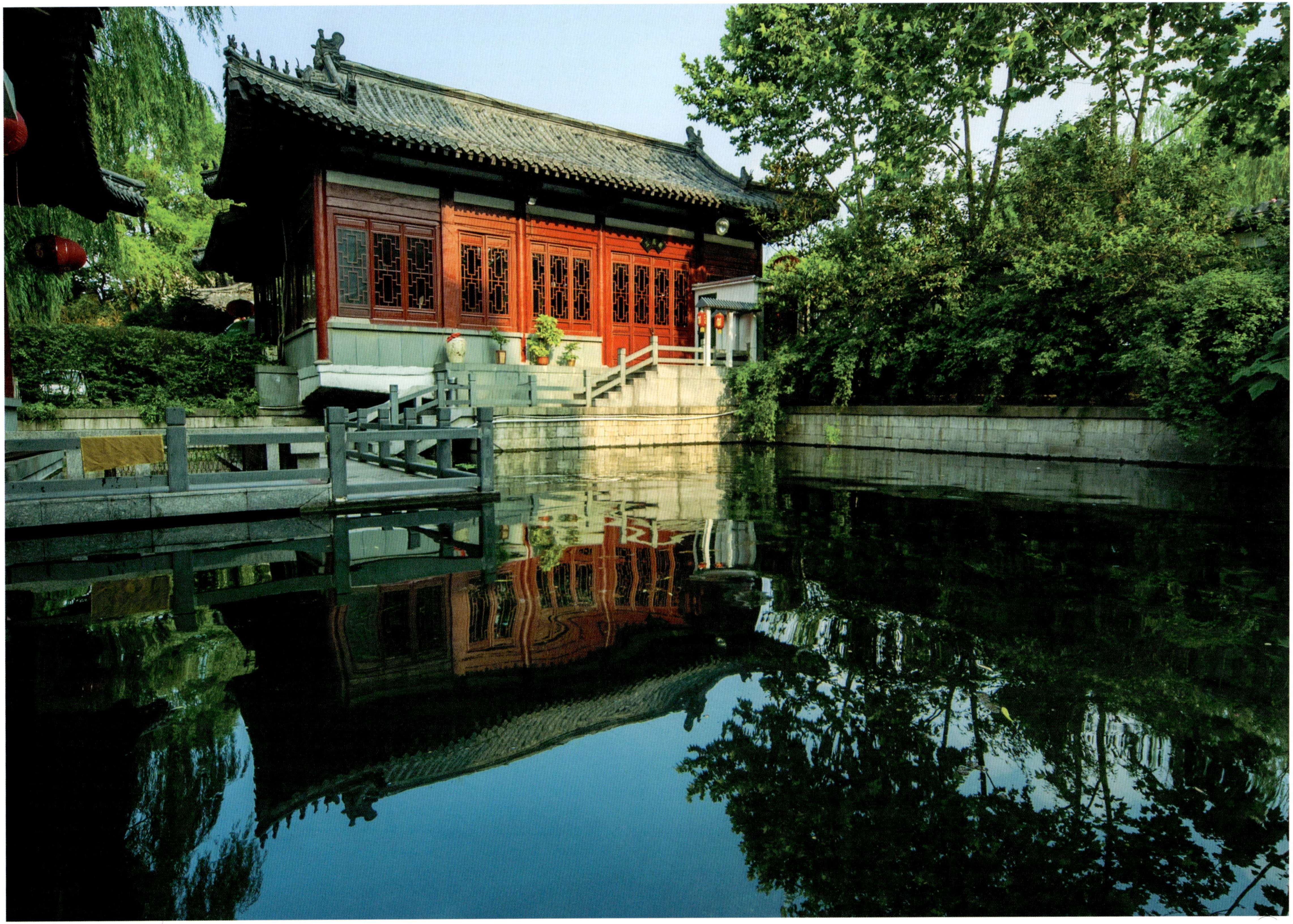

柳荫凉，
影婆娑，
月照蓝池约略。
一碗酒，
半炷香，
夜寂面冷霜。
石磐座，
三更桥，
泉水汩流破月。
屏住气，
静心听，
物我互语声。

王化学《更漏子·月牙泉》

月牙泉

月牙泉，最早因其一弯泉水形似新月而得名。据文献记载，月牙泉"水极清澈。有王氏宅临泉，隔一墙，内有巨池，蓄红鱼数十头，长几尺余，粗如巨桶，不知养自何年"。（清·王培荀《乡园忆旧录》）该泉位于五龙潭公园东南隅，古温泉东。

Yueya Spring

The spring was named Yueya because its shape is like a crescent moon. According to literature, Yueya Spring is "extremely clean. The Wangs' house is beside the spring, just separated by a wall. The house has a big pool with dozens of red fish, which are inches long and as thick as buckets. No one knows how long they have been kept." (Wang Peixun, the Qing Dynasty, *A Memoir of Village Garden*) It is in the southeast corner of Wulong Spring Park, and to the east of Guwen Park.

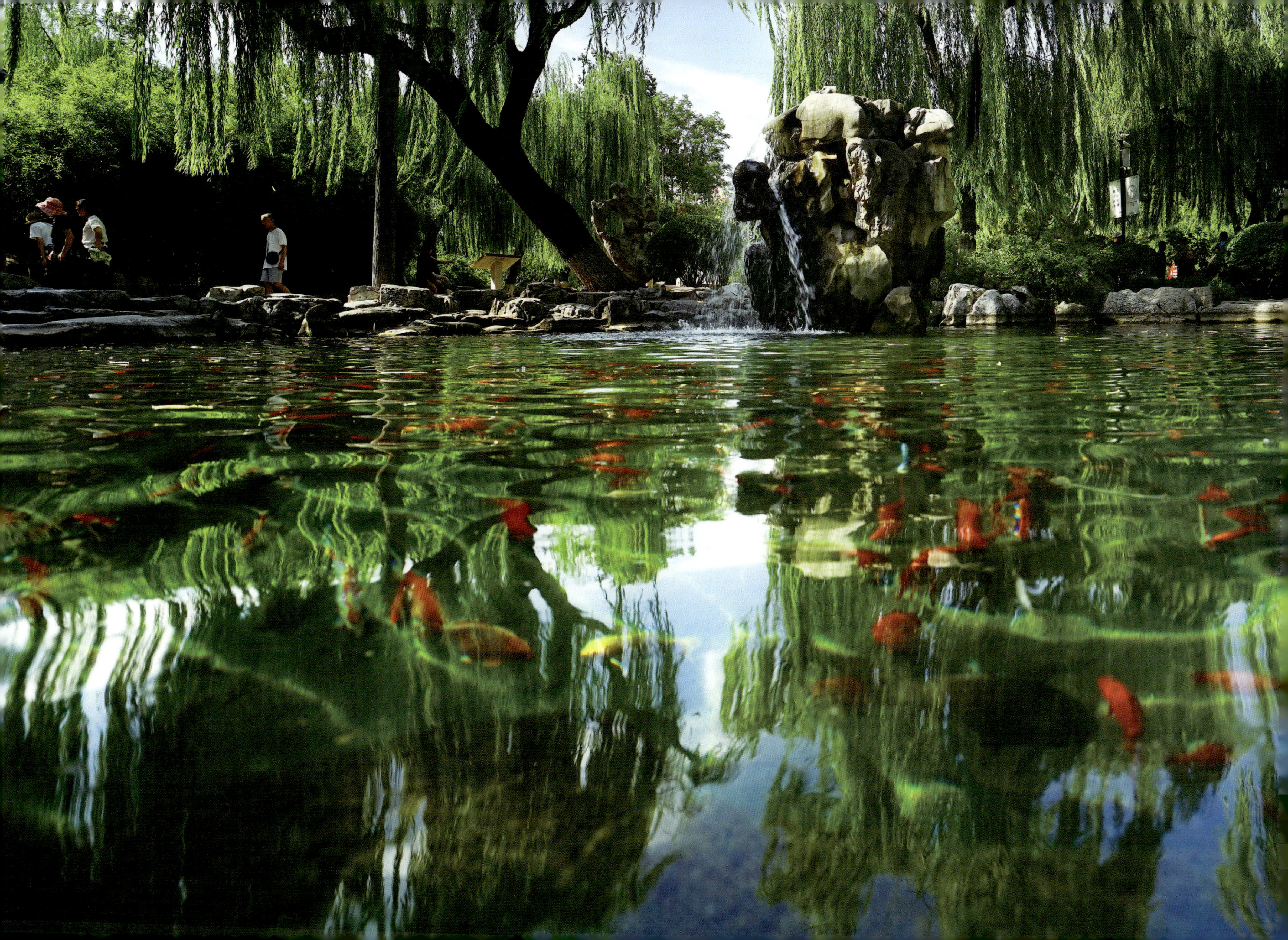

西池泉味比东强，何必天寒割蜜房。莫道脂甘能悦口，试将一饮胜天浆。

（明）晏璧《济南七十二泉诗》

西蜜脂泉

Ximizhi Spring

The spring was given the name Mizhi (honey) for the sweet taste of its water. On the west side of the south gate of Wulong Park is Ximizhi Spring; on the east side is the Dongmizhi Spring. As a poem described, "The rippling stream connects the eastern and the western springs, both of which are named Mizhi." (Yan Bi, the Ming Dynasty, *Dongmizhi Spring*)

蜜脂泉，意为其泉水甘甜如蜜。在五龙潭公园南门西侧的蜜脂泉被称为"西蜜脂泉"，东侧的蜜脂泉被称为"东蜜脂泉"。古人有诗赞颂曰："清泉流出碧涟漪，脉贯东西号蜜脂。说着到头辛苦处，谁知滋味美如饴。"（明·晏璧《东蜜脂泉》）

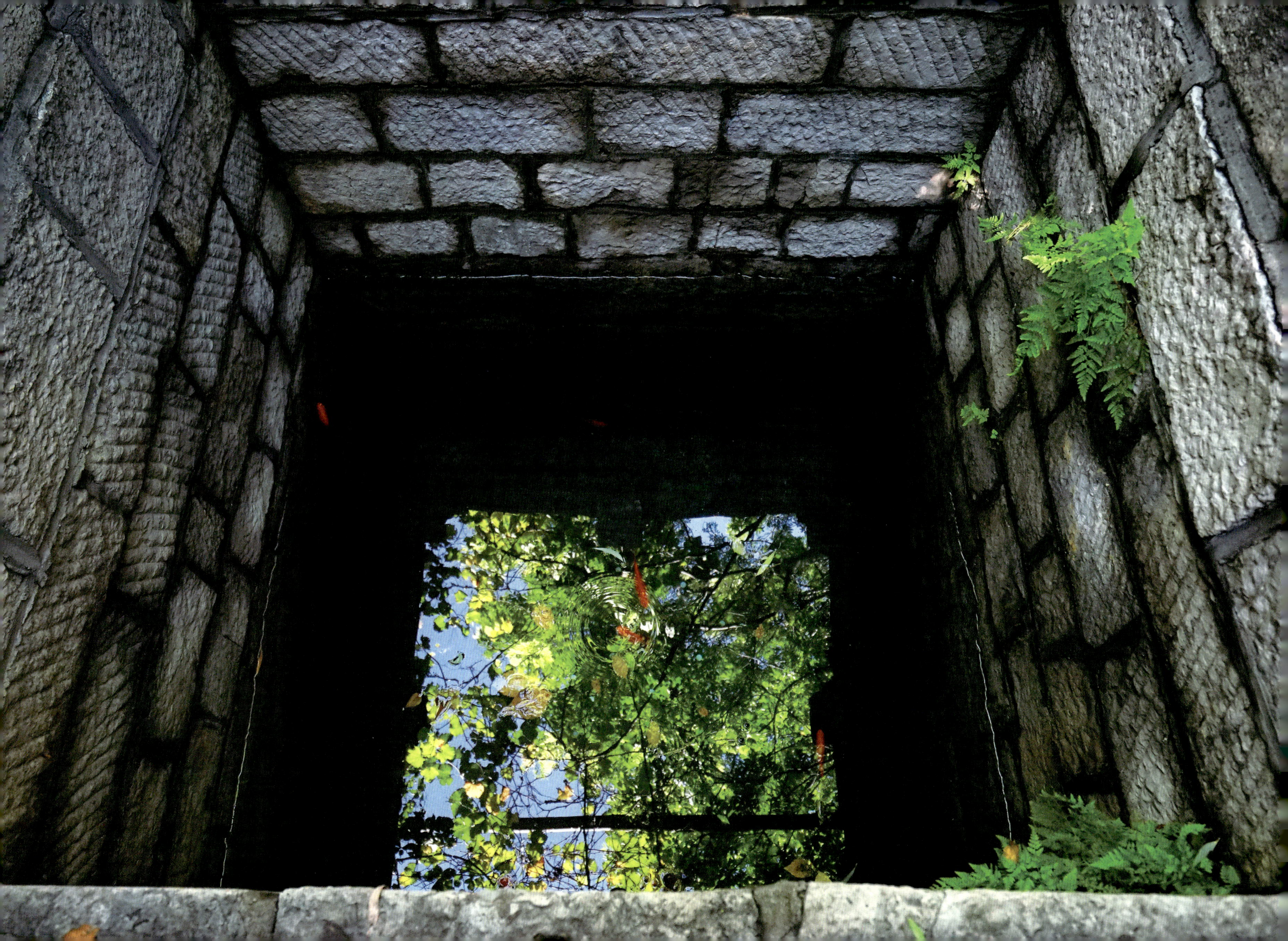

Guanjia Pond

The water of Guanjia Pond is clean and cool. Ever since old days, local people have been raising bean sprouts here. It also supplies drinking water for the nearby inhabitants. Green willows and bamboos, a small bridge and lively fishes contribute to the charming scenery. It is a good place for leisure and worth visiting. It is to the northwest of Wulong Pond.

官家池

官家池泉眼众多，水质清冽，自古以来，就是当地百姓泡生豆芽的地方，也是附近居民的饮用水源。泉池周围绿柳夹岸，茅亭立竹，小桥卧波，锦鱼戏水，风光旖旎，环境十分优美，是一处休闲观光的好去处。该池位于五龙潭的水潭西北处。

泉隶五龙潭，
官家池瞰然。
周边花锦簇，
自然石驳岸。
水沛无绝期，
早年亦难干。
街坊邻居爱，
世代共甘甜。

王化学《官家池》

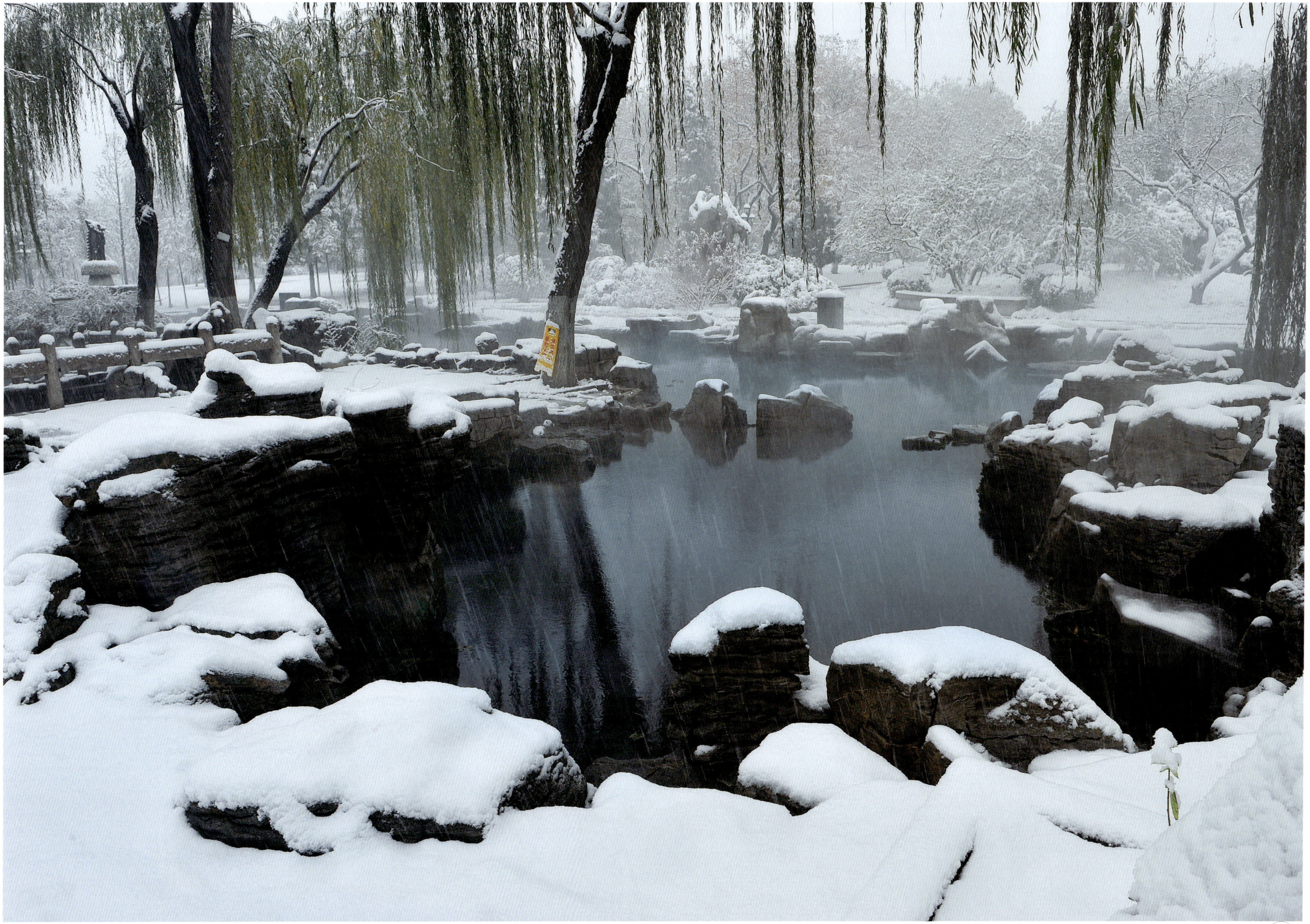

初唐秦叔宝，
宅第五龙潭。
晨起遛战马，
蹄腾踏此泉。
池宽水势旺，
泽润一方田。
游客凭栏赏，
传说添内涵。

王化学《回马泉》

回马泉

相传，唐朝开国名将秦琼在济南为武时，手持双锏，骑一匹高头大马，追赶贼人至此并与之交战。鏖战中，秦琼所骑战马猛一回首，因蹄力过猛，马蹄落处竟踏出一泓清泉。济南人为纪念秦琼，遂将此泉命名为"回马泉"。该泉位于五龙潭的水潭东南处，古温泉西，水绕亭台廊榭。

Huima Spring

According to a folk story, the famous general Qin Qiong of the Tang Dynasty was once chasing and fighting with burglars in Jinan. He was using double mace and riding a horse. In the battle, his horse suddenly turned back. The horse was using so much strength on feet that the land was sunk by the hooves and a spring gushed out. In order to memorize Qin Qiong, people named the spring Huima (a turning back horse). It is to the southeast of Wulong Pond, to the west of Guwen Pond, and surrounding pavilions, terraces, porches and sheds.

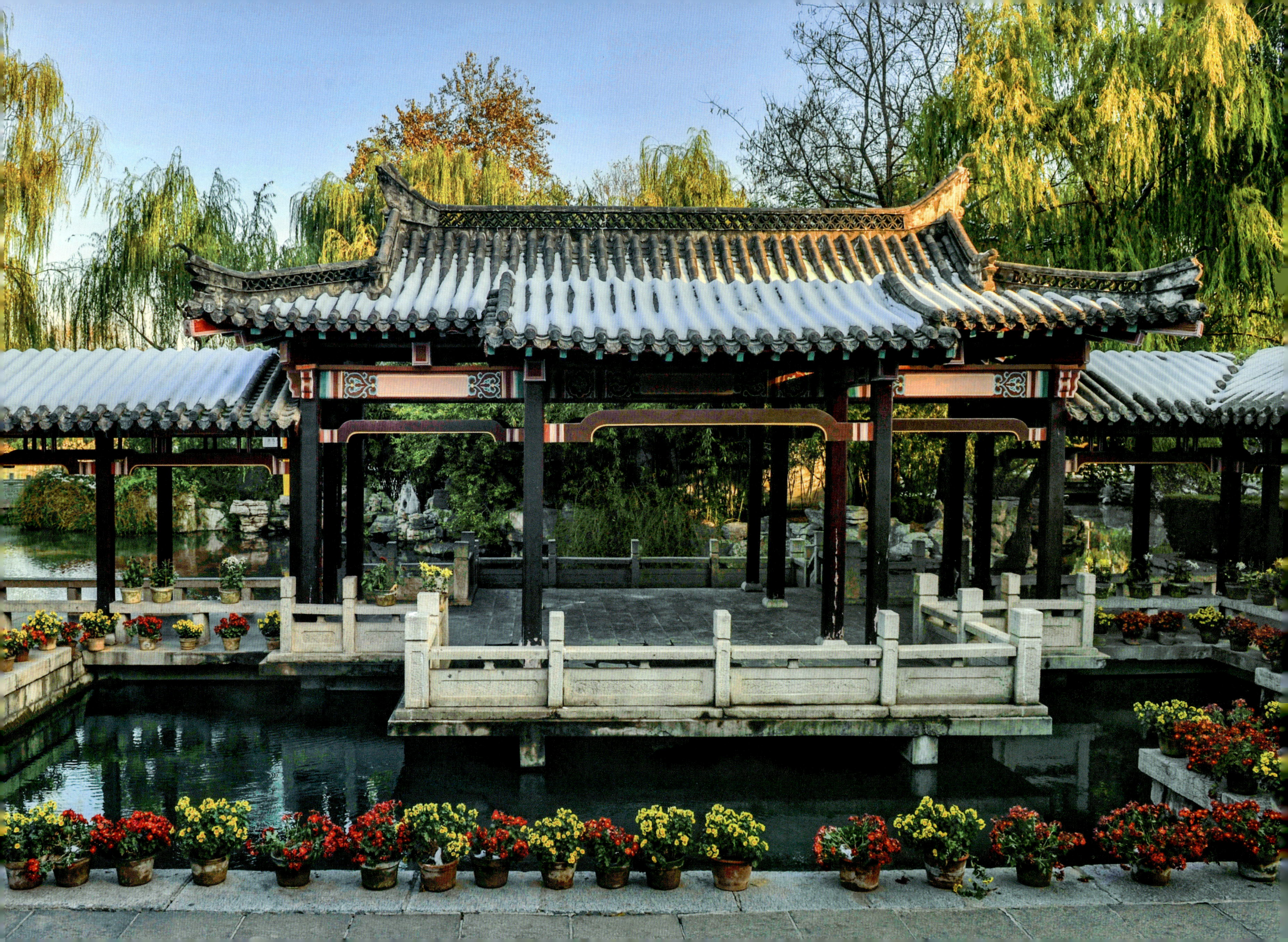

草木修竹庇荫之，
此泉涌奔乱石矶。
水花喷吐虬龙貌，
得是名扬胜香溪。
王化学《虬溪泉》

虬溪泉

因水流喷出后，犹如古代传说中头生双角的虬龙盘曲吐水一般，故而得名"虬溪泉"。1965年相关地质部门进行钻探实验时，钻孔中突然喷出泉水，而且涌流不止，水势浩大，故将此处作为泉眼保留至今，这是"新七十二泉"中比较年轻的泉眼之一。该泉位于五龙潭公园内的月牙泉东北侧。

Qiuxi Spring

The streams spew out, just like an ancient double-horned dragon spits water, so it was named "Qiuxi" (dragon stream). It is one of the youngest springs in the "Newly Selected 72 Famous Springs". In 1965, when a geological department was doing drilling experiment, the spring suddenly spewed out. The water is constant and abundant, so it has been kept since then. It is to the northeast of Yueya Spring in Wulong Pond Park.

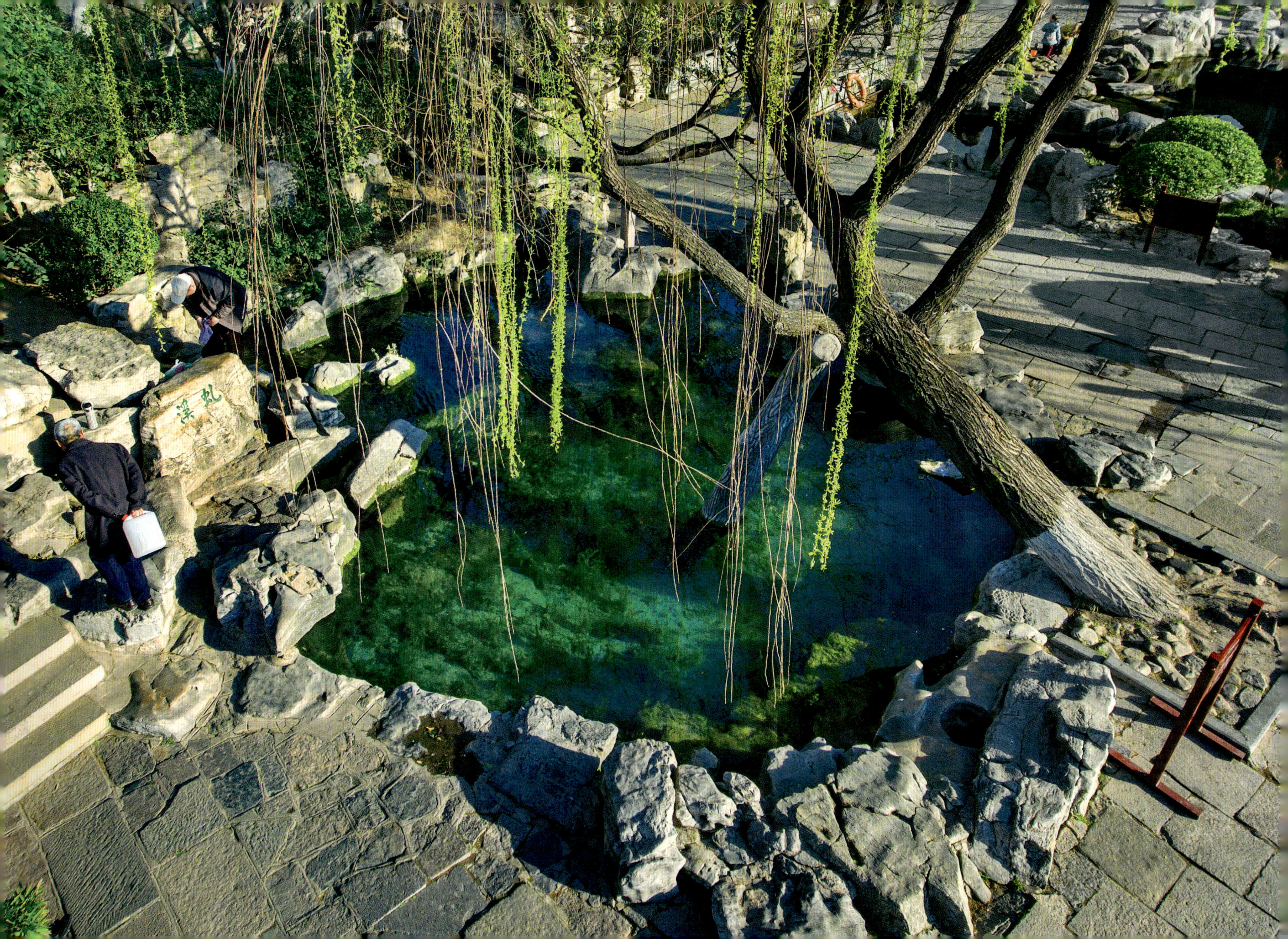

玉泉

此泉因泉水清澈见底,晶莹剔透,宛如翠玉而得名。玉泉与虬溪泉一样,系地质钻探而发现的年轻泉眼。泉水自池底涌出,沿水溪蜿蜒东流,泉池系自然石砌垒而成。游客可俯身汲饮,为人们喜爱的亲水之地。该泉位于五龙潭东南,回马泉北。

Yu Spring

The water is crystal clear, just like a jade, so the spring was named Yu (jade). Like Qiuxi Spring, it is a young spring formed by geological drilling. The water spews out from the bottom of the pool, and wanders eastward in a brook. It is very attractive for visitors because they can bend down and drink its water. It is to the southeast of Wulong Spring and to the north of Huima Spring.

晓行坐爱碧玉澜,
别有洞天胜江南。
尘心俱此豁然朗,
白云长在水涟涟。

拾荒《晨漫步玉泉歌》

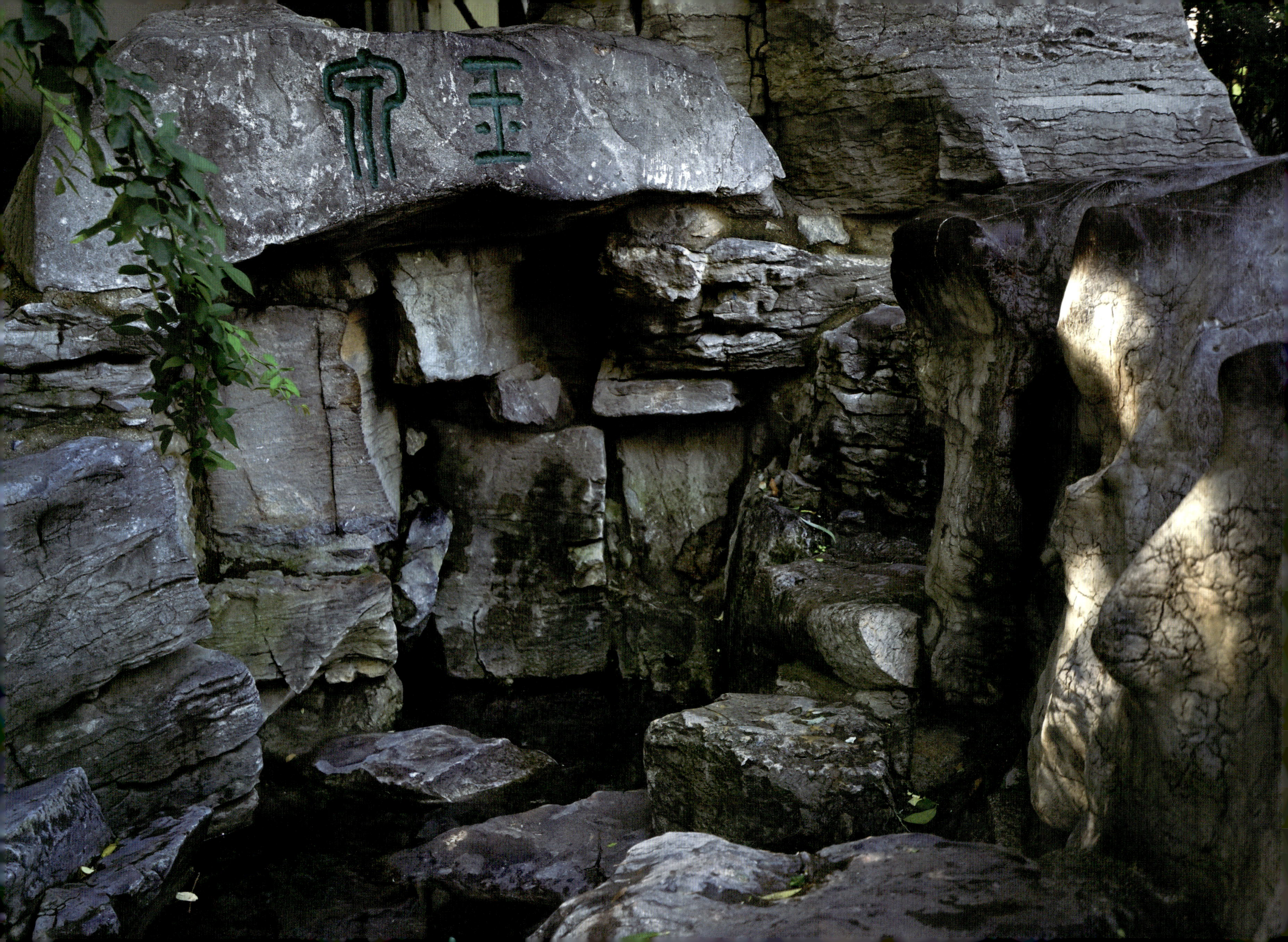

濂泉

此泉因泉水既平静又清澈，遂命名为"濂泉"。旧时因有陈姓人家居住于泉旁，所以又俗称"陈家池子"。濂泉虽然没有奋涌若轮的磅礴气势，却因无数涓涓细流从池底不停涌出，漫溢石板路上，形成"清泉石上流"的景观而深受游客喜爱。该泉位于五龙潭公园西隅，官家池西北。

Lian Spring

In the past, a Chen family lived beside the spring for several generations, so it was called Chenjia Pond. Later in a general survey on famous springs, it was named Lian (smooth water). Although the water of the spring is not strong, its constant trickle overflows the stone path, which is a unique scenery beloved by visitors. It is in the west corner of Wulong Park and to the northwest of Guanjia Pond.

濂轩翼翼水清清，青石板上濯泠泠。我欲解襟笔一字，又恐寒泉把诗凝。

拾荒《濂泉寄情》

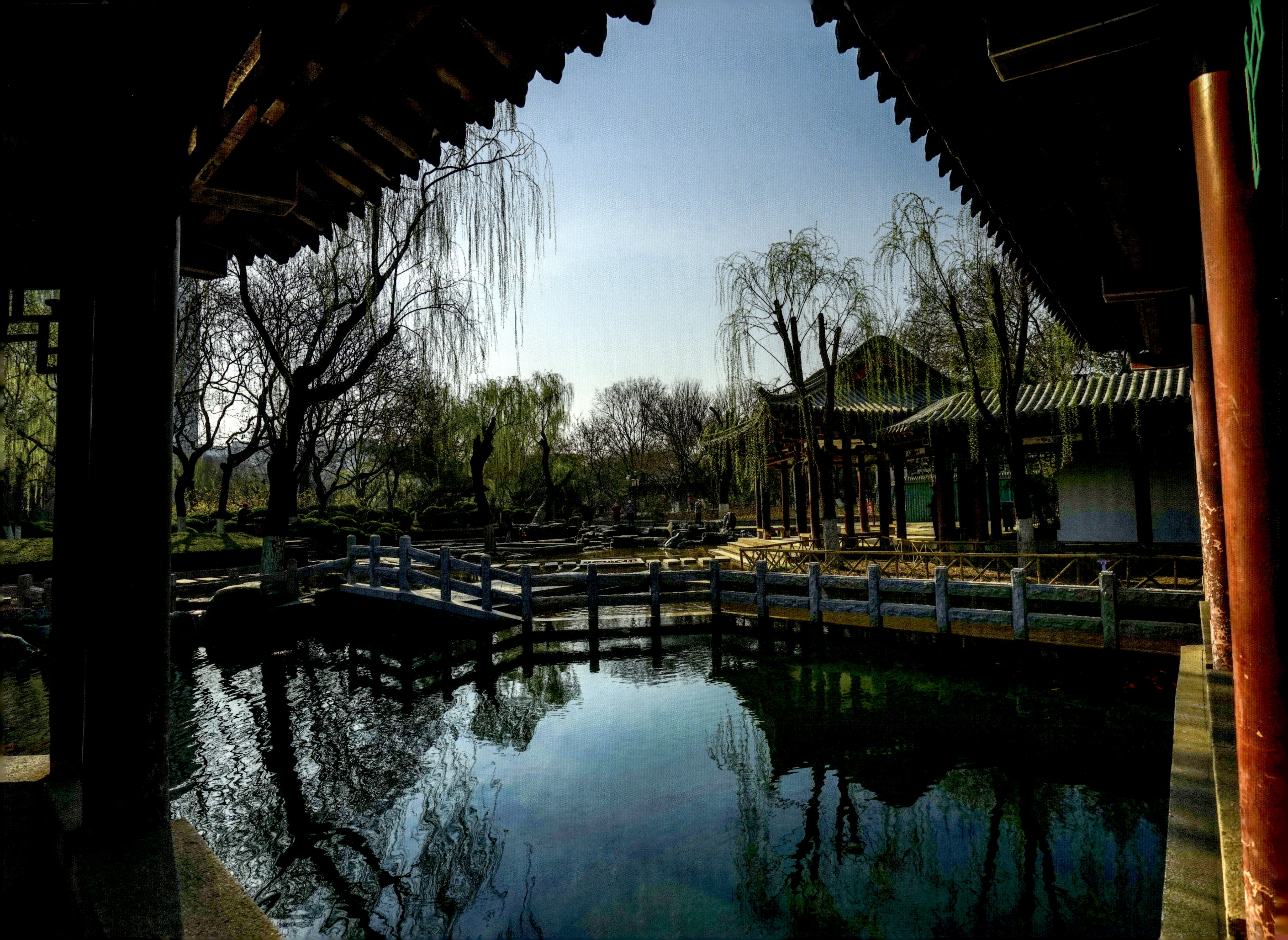

Jinan:
A City Enriched by Famous Springs

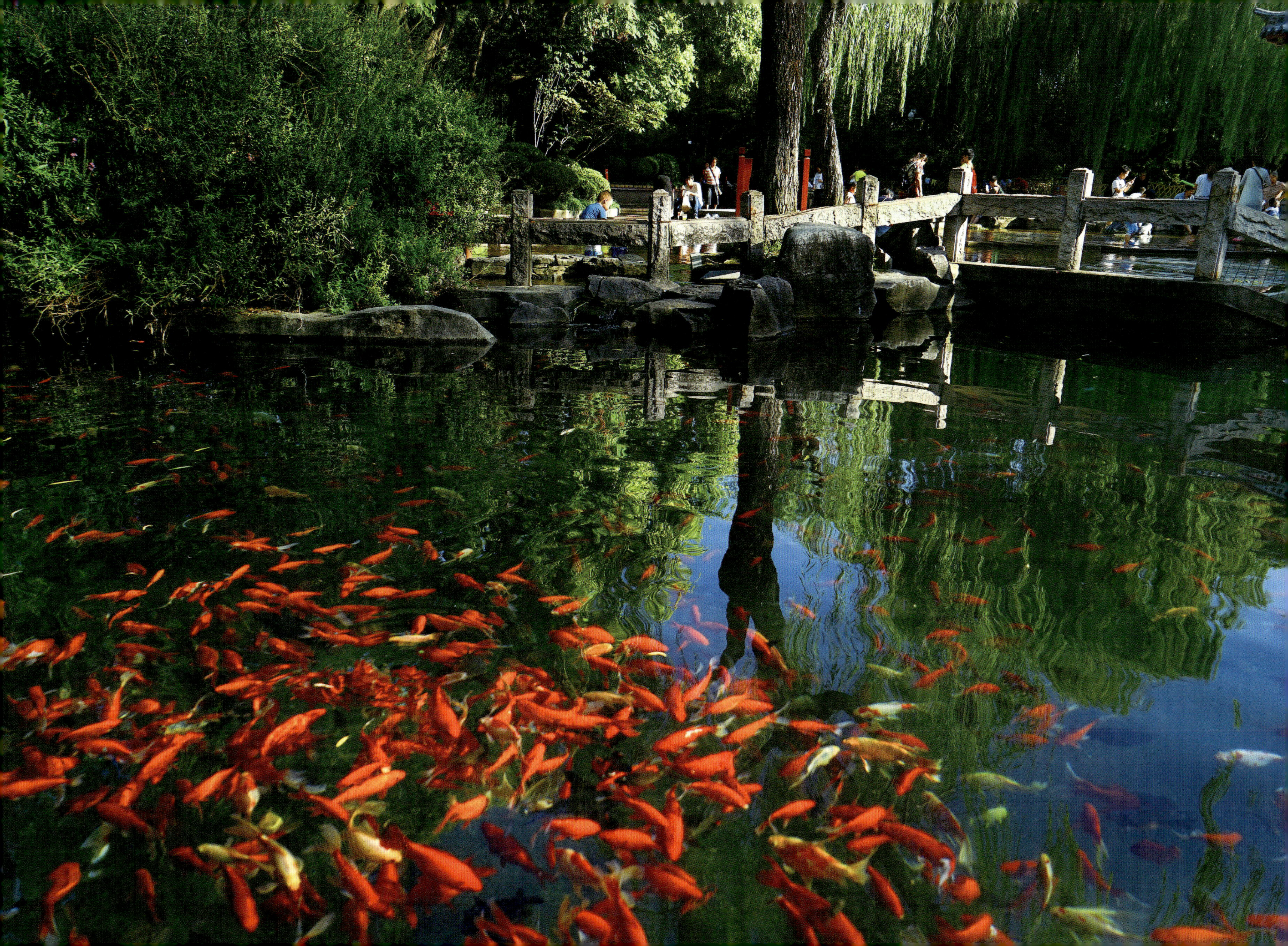

Jinan:
A City Enriched by Famous Springs

其他
名泉

Other Famous Springs

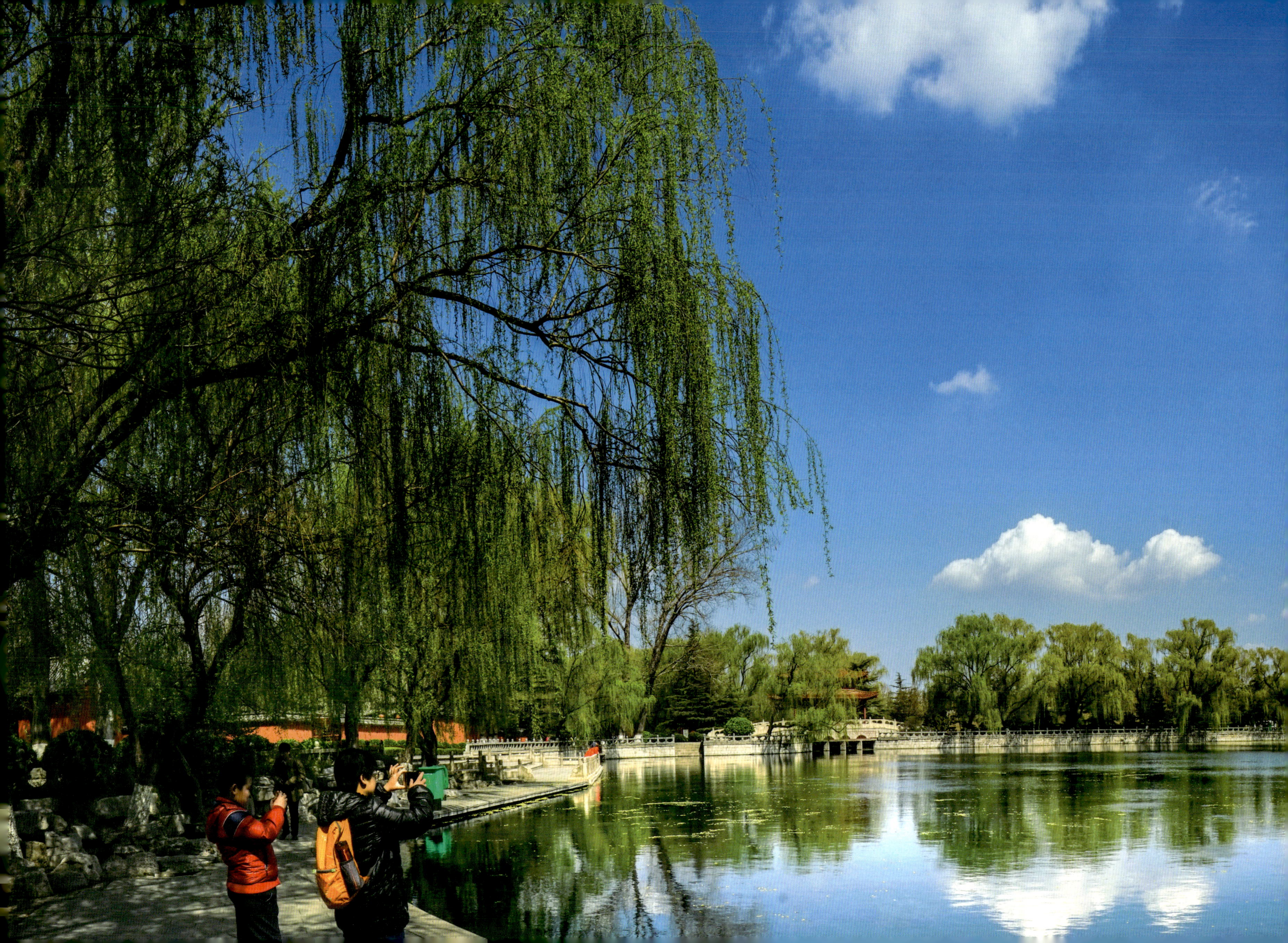

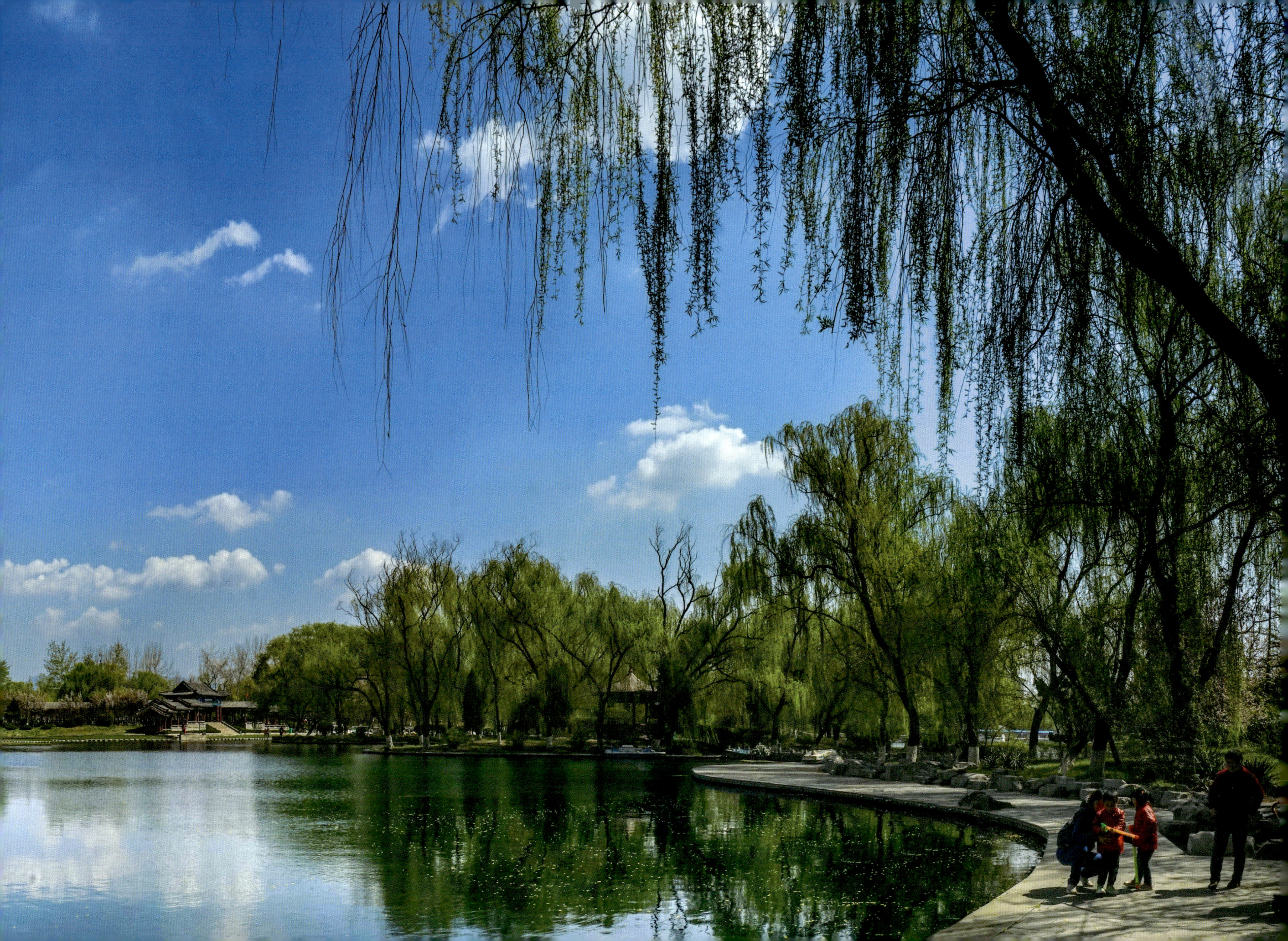

The Other Famous Springs

There are ten spring groups, including more than eight hundred springs in Jinan. Besides the four spring groups mentioned above, there are Bai Spring Group, Yong Spring Group, Yuhe Spring Group, Baimai Spring Group, Jiasha Spring Group, and Hongfan Pond Spring Group. These spring groups are distributed in Eastern Suburbs, Southern Mountain Area, Caishi and Ganggou districts in the East, Mingshui in Zhangqiu, the Upper and Middle Reaches of Langxi River in Pingyin, etc. Except the springs of the ten groups, there are many springs scattered in counties of Jinan.

The following are the springs of the other groups that belong to the "Newly Selected 72 Famous Springs":

Bai Spring and Hua Spring in Bai Spring Group;

Yong Spring, Kuju Spring, Bishu Spring, Tu Spring, Niyu Spring, Da Spring, Shengshui Spring and Duanhua Spring in Yong Spring Group;

Yuhe Spring in Yuhe Spring Group;

Baimai Spring, Dongma Inlet, Xima Inlet, Mo Spring, Meihua Spring, Jingming Spring in Baimai Spring Group;

Jiasha Spring, Zhuoxi Spring, Qingling Spring, Tanbao Spring, Xiaolu Spring in Jiasha Spring Group;

Hongfan Pond, Shuyuan Spring, Hu Spring, Riyue Spring in Hongfan Pond Spring Group;

Another 6 scattered springs, namely, Jiangshui Spring, Yan Pond, Ganlu Spring, Linji Spring, Doumu Spring and Wuying Pond, are also among the "Newly Selected 72 Famous Springs".

其他名泉

济南总计有十大泉群，八百余处泉眼。除前述四大泉群外，还有白泉泉群、涌泉泉群、玉河泉泉群、百脉泉泉群、袈裟泉泉群和洪范池泉群。这些泉群分别分布在济南东郊，南部山区，济南东部彩石、港沟一带，章丘明水和平阴浪溪河中上游等地。除十大泉群所属泉眼外，还有许多散泉分布在济南各县区。

其他泉群中，白泉泉群的白泉、华泉2处，涌泉泉群的涌泉、苦苣泉、避暑泉、突泉、泥淤泉、大泉、圣水泉、缎华泉8处，玉河泉泉群的玉河泉1处，百脉泉泉群的百脉泉、东麻湾、西麻湾、墨泉、梅花泉、净明泉6处，袈裟泉泉群的袈裟泉、卓锡泉、清泠泉、檀抱泉、晓露泉5处，洪范池泉群的洪范池、书院泉、扈泉、日月泉4处，其他散泉如浆水泉、砚池、甘露泉、林汲泉、斗母泉、无影潭等6处，均在"新七十二名泉"之列。

Hua Spring

Hua Spring is one of the earliest springs which appeared in ancient Chinese literature. It was named Hua because it was at the foot of Mount Hua. In 589 B.C., a war between the Qi army and the Jin army broke out in Mount Ma'an. The Qi army was totally defeated and chased by the Jin army around Mount Hua. A senior official of Qi named Pang choufu came up with a good idea at the crucial time. He asked the Monarch of Qi to disguise himself and pretend to get water from Hua Spring. The Monarch followed his scheme and finally fled. Ever since then, Hua Spring have frequently been recorded in the literature of successive dynasties. It is in the northeast of Jinan city, in front of the Huayang Palace in Huashan National Historical and Cultural Park.

华泉

华泉是最早见于中国古代文献的济南名泉之一，因地处华山脚下而得名。相传，公元前589年，齐、晋两军大战于马鞍山，齐军溃败，被晋军追得"三周华不注"。齐国大夫逢丑父急中生智，让齐顷公化装后假借去华泉汲水之机得以逃脱。自此，华泉在历代典籍中多有记载。该泉位于济南市区东北，华山国家历史文化公园华阳宫前。

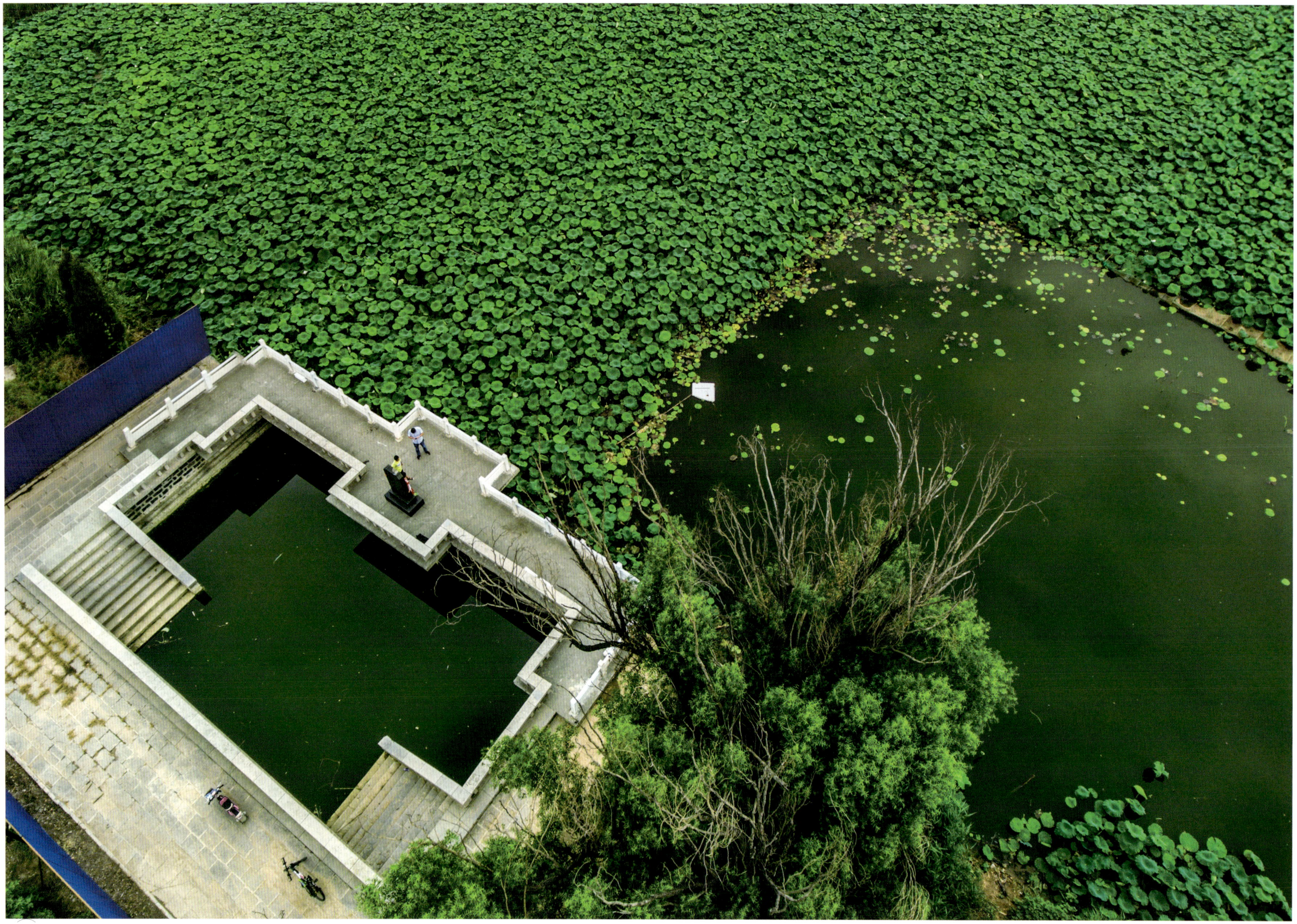

虎牙千仞立巉巉，
峻拔遥临济水南。
翠岭嫩岚晴可掇，
金舆陈迹久谁探。
高标特起青云近，
壮士三周战气酣。
丑父遗忠无处问，
空余一掬野泉甘。

（宋）曾巩《华不注山》

甘露泉

> 味同甘露冷同冰,
> 大佛山头一勺清。
> 不信此泉堪煮茗,
> 拭苔拂草看题名。
> 〔清〕任弘远《甘露泉》

甘露泉亦称试茶泉、秋棠池、滴露泉,泉水享有"味甘却似饮天浆"之盛誉,尤其适合烹茶。过去,常有文人墨客居此读书品茗。因泉畔生有多株秋海棠,枝叶茂盛,每逢花季,如火如荼,花落池中,色如胭脂,故又称"秋棠池"。该泉位于济南千佛山东南的佛慧山峰下深涧内,开元寺遗址南侧山崖下。

Ganlu Spring

The spring is also called Shicha Spring, Qiutang Pond and Dilu Spring. The water is extremely sweet and good for making tea. In the past, men of letters often lived beside the spring, reading books and drinking tea. There are several begonias beside the spring. That's why the spring is also called Qiutang Spring. In blooming time, the flowers are red as a raging fire. When the petals fall into the pool, they became rouge-red. It is part of a deep stream under Fohui Mountain which is to the southeast of Qianfo Mountain, and below the south cliff of Kaiyuan Temple.

命如泉湧

无影潭

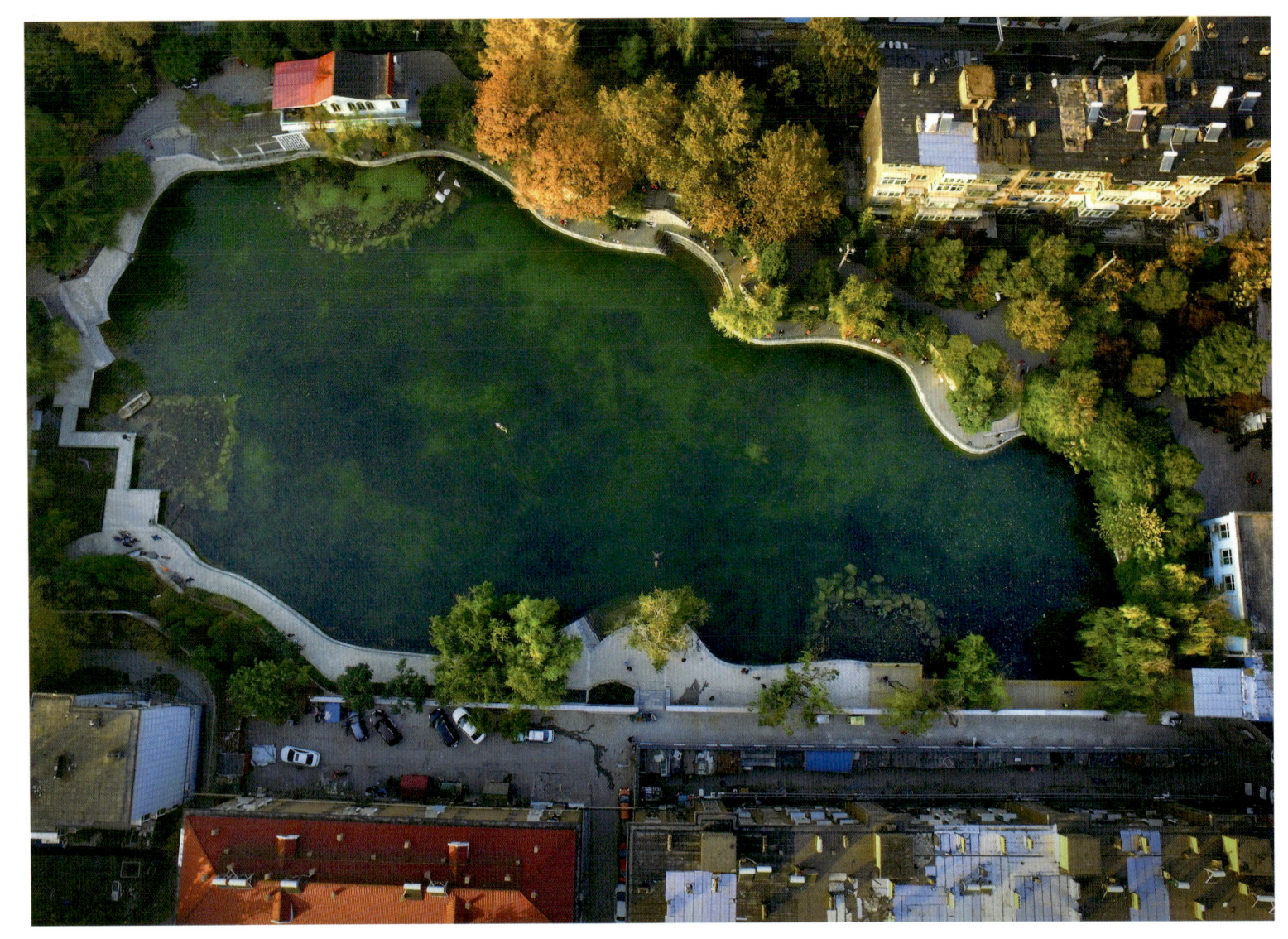

无影潭因地处无影山而得名。泉因多年挖沙逐渐形成，水由潭底诸多细微岩孔涌出，积水成塘，常年不涸。泉池以石砌岸，四周绿树摇碧，芦苇丛生，北岸设有船坞，供游客乘船游览。该潭位于济南天桥区无影山路和无影山中路交叉口东南。

Wuying Pond

The spring follows the name of the hill where it is located. The spring came out of years' work of digging sand. The water spews out from many tiny stone holes and forms a big pond. The reedy pond is surrounded by green trees on the stone-made banks. There is a dock on the north bank, providing boat service for visitors. It is to the southeast of the crossing of Wuyingshan Road and Wuyingshanzhong Road in Tianqiao District.

岸边杨柳荫，
水面漂微皱。
棹楫弄苔藓，
风雨突来骤。
雨歇碧苍苍，
无影潭谁顾？
寂寥更淡然，
蝉噪蛙声后。

王化学《生查子·无影潭》

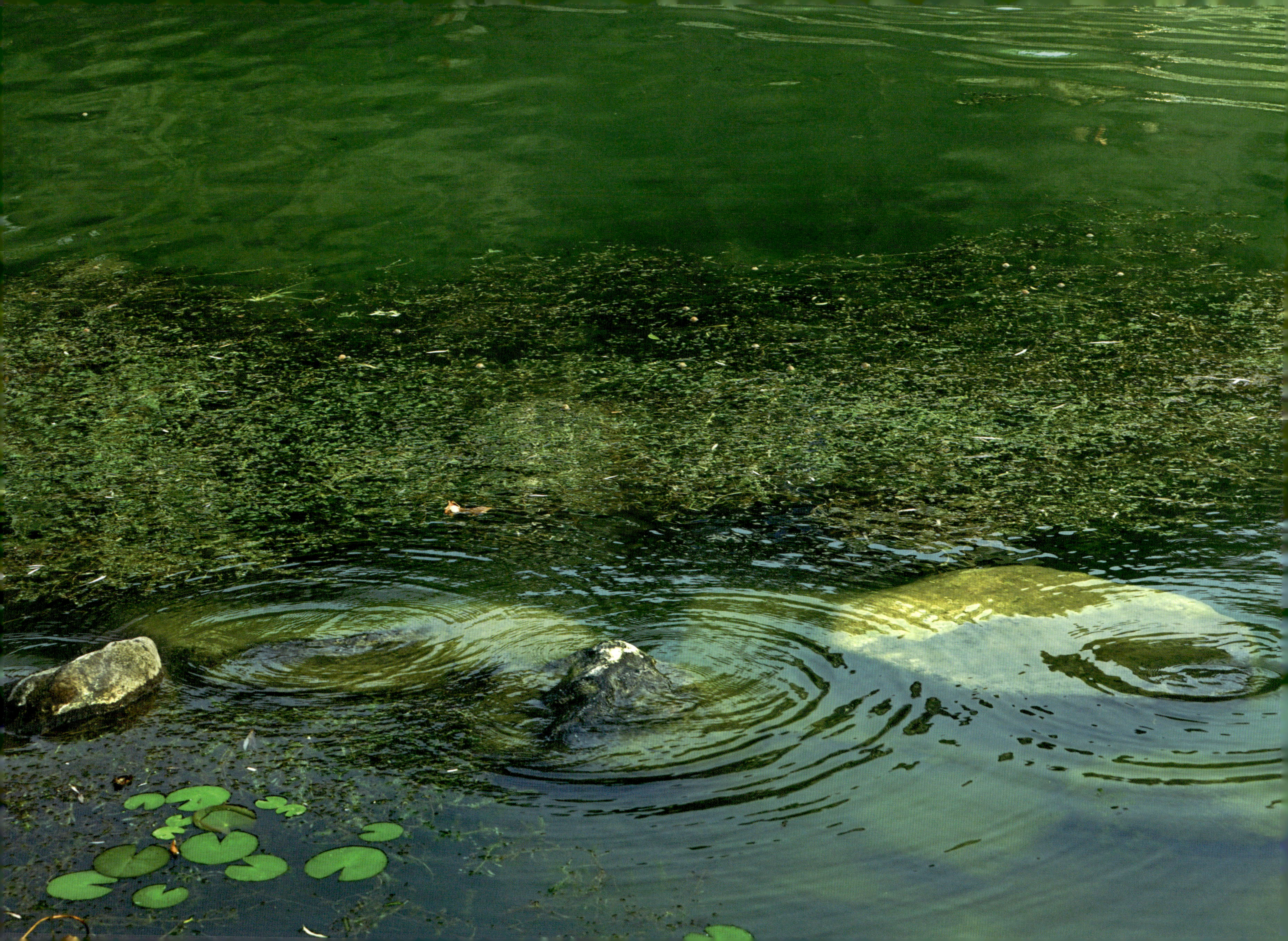

涌泉

Yong Spring

The water spills out through the gaps between the rocks on the hillside. When the water overflows the pool, it pours down along the hillside, forming a waterfall which is nearly a 100m high. The spring is surrounded by a number of tall bamboos and flagrant flowers. The water makes clanks by beating the rocks. Mist and cloud curl up to the hill, making it a fairyland. It is in the southwest of Simen Pagoda scenic spot in Liubu Town of Licheng District, and below the south side of Baihu Mountain.

涌泉因水从山腰岩溶缝隙中涌出而得名。泉水溢满泉池后，沿山势三跌而下，形成落差近百米的瀑布。周边修竹千竿，鸟语花香，水击岩石，铮铮作响，山光烟岚，洵为胜地。该泉位于济南市历城区柳埠村四门塔景区西南，白虎山南麓。

锦阳川上女僧家,
红树萧萧白日斜。
弟子如云人不见,
可怜秋老玉莲花。
〔明〕李攀龙《浦泉庵》

避暑泉

避暑泉一名，首见于明代《历城县志》，得天独厚的地理环境，使这里在盛夏时节仍旧十分凉爽，适合人们来此避暑，故而得名"避暑泉"。泉水由两个洞口流出，汇入半圆形的自然水湾之中。盛水期，泉水漫溢，沿山溪蜿蜒而下。该泉位于柳埠镇袁洪峪南岭西侧山坳间。

Bishu Spring

Its name is derived from *The Annals of Licheng County*. Because of its advantaged geographical conditions, it is still cool in midsummer beside the spring. Therefore, the spring was named Bishu (avoid summer heat). The water flows from two holes and converges into a semicircle inlet. When the water is abundant, it overflows and winds down in a mountain stream. It is in the west col of the south ridge of Yuanhong Valley in Liubu Town.

> 山坳处落平湖，茂林珠。
> 夏日清凉避酷任踯躅。
> 甜桃硕，白云朵，鸟翻飞，
> 借问桃源世外尔为谁？
> 王化学《相见欢·避暑泉》

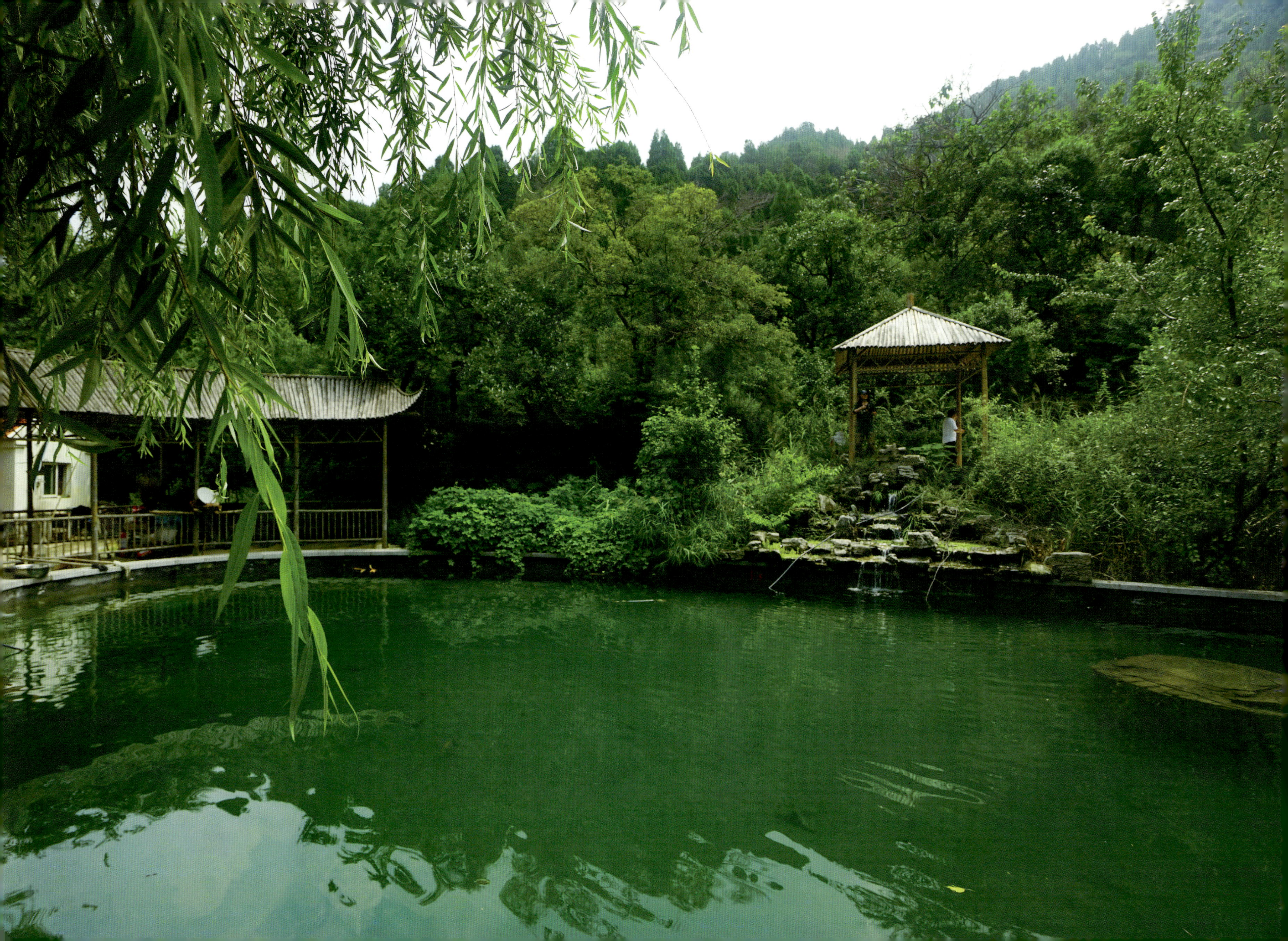

圣水,
圣水,
背靠龙山茸翠。
涓涓洞穴涌流,
兴教经声夜幽。
幽夜,
幽夜,
古树苍碑灰色。

王化学《调笑令·圣水泉》

圣水泉

古时,济南南部山区佛教十分兴盛,建有多处寺庙,位于寺庙周边的泉池便被称为"圣水泉",据说饮其泉水可延年益寿。所以,南部山区以"圣水"而命名的名泉就有多处。这里的圣水泉位于红叶谷风景区内海拔575米山坡上的一处自然洞穴中,泉池漫溢后,泉水顺山势流下。

Shengshui Spring

In the past, Buddhism was prosperous in the Southern Mountain Area of Jinan, and many temples were built there. Since temples are sacred Buddhist places, the springs near the temples are also considered sacred. It is said that people who drink the spring water can extend life span. Therefore, there are many springs named Shengshui (sacred water). The Shengshui Spring mentioned here is the one located in a cave on a 575m-high mountain, which is in Red Leaf Valley scenic spot. Its water overflows and streams down the mountain.

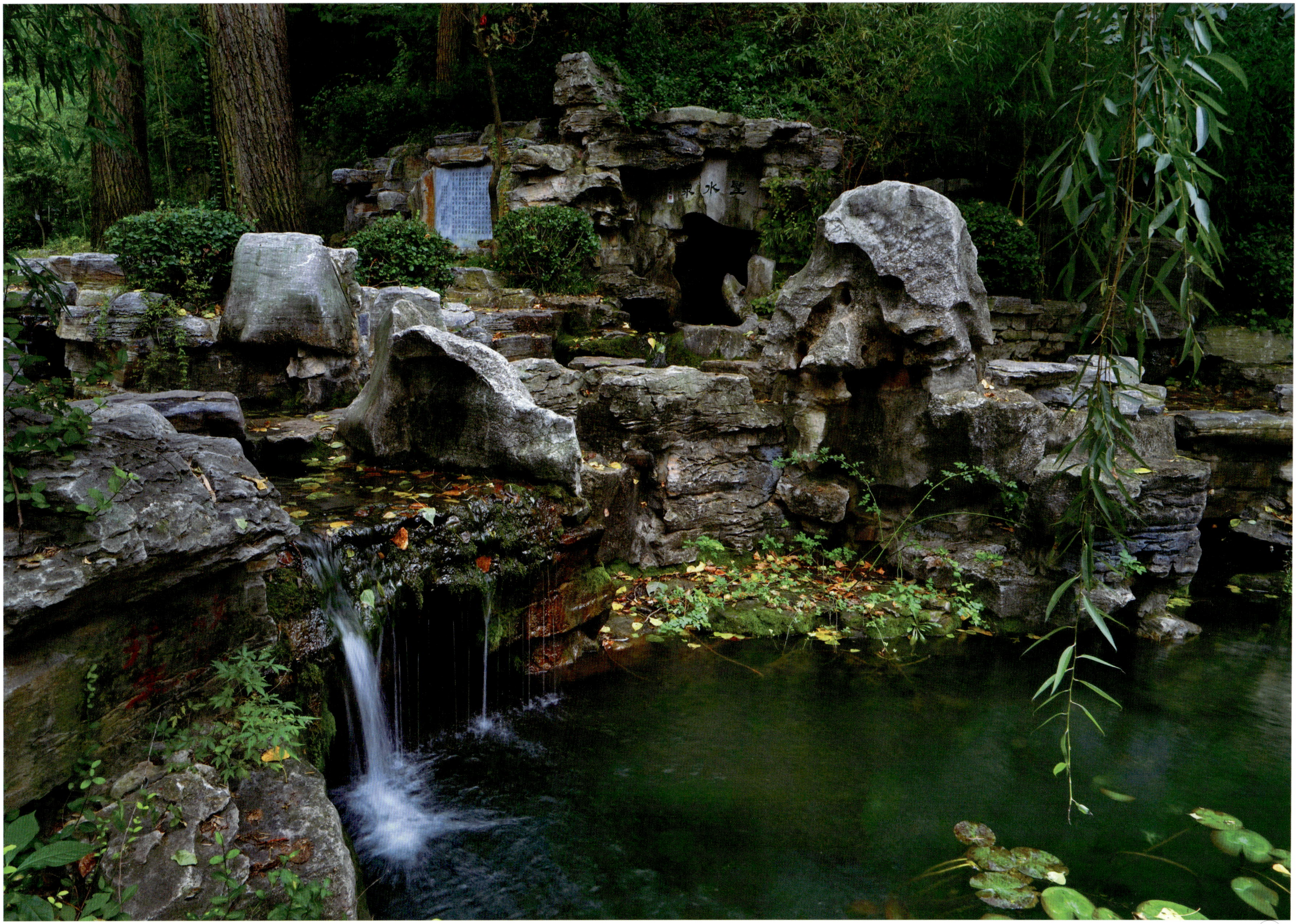
望水泉

缎华泉

缎华泉，因其清泉平静如缎、水纹涟漪如华而得名。泉旁有一古井，是缎华泉的泉源。古井终年涌水，使缎华泉可以久旱不涸。该泉位于九顶塔风景区内。

Duanhua Spring

The spring looks as smooth as satin, and its ripples look like blooming flowers. Therefore, it was named Duanhua (satin and flower). The nearby old well is the water source of the spring. The well keeps water all the year round. The spring is located in Jiuding Temple scenic spot.

九塔寺阳有缎华，
泉池荡漾泛白花。
扶栏望透鱼浅底，
绿缎彩锦似流霞。

王化学《缎华泉》

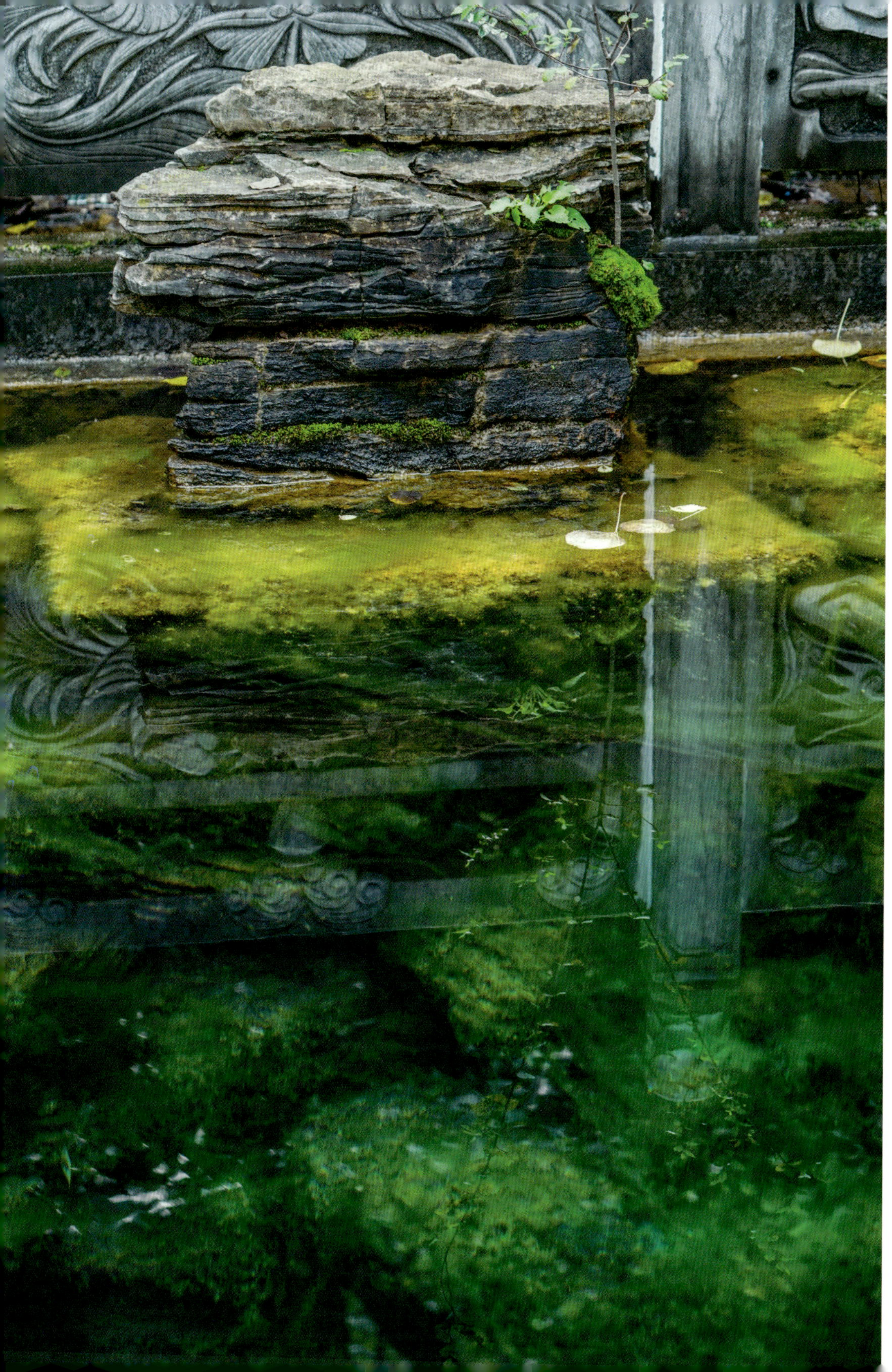
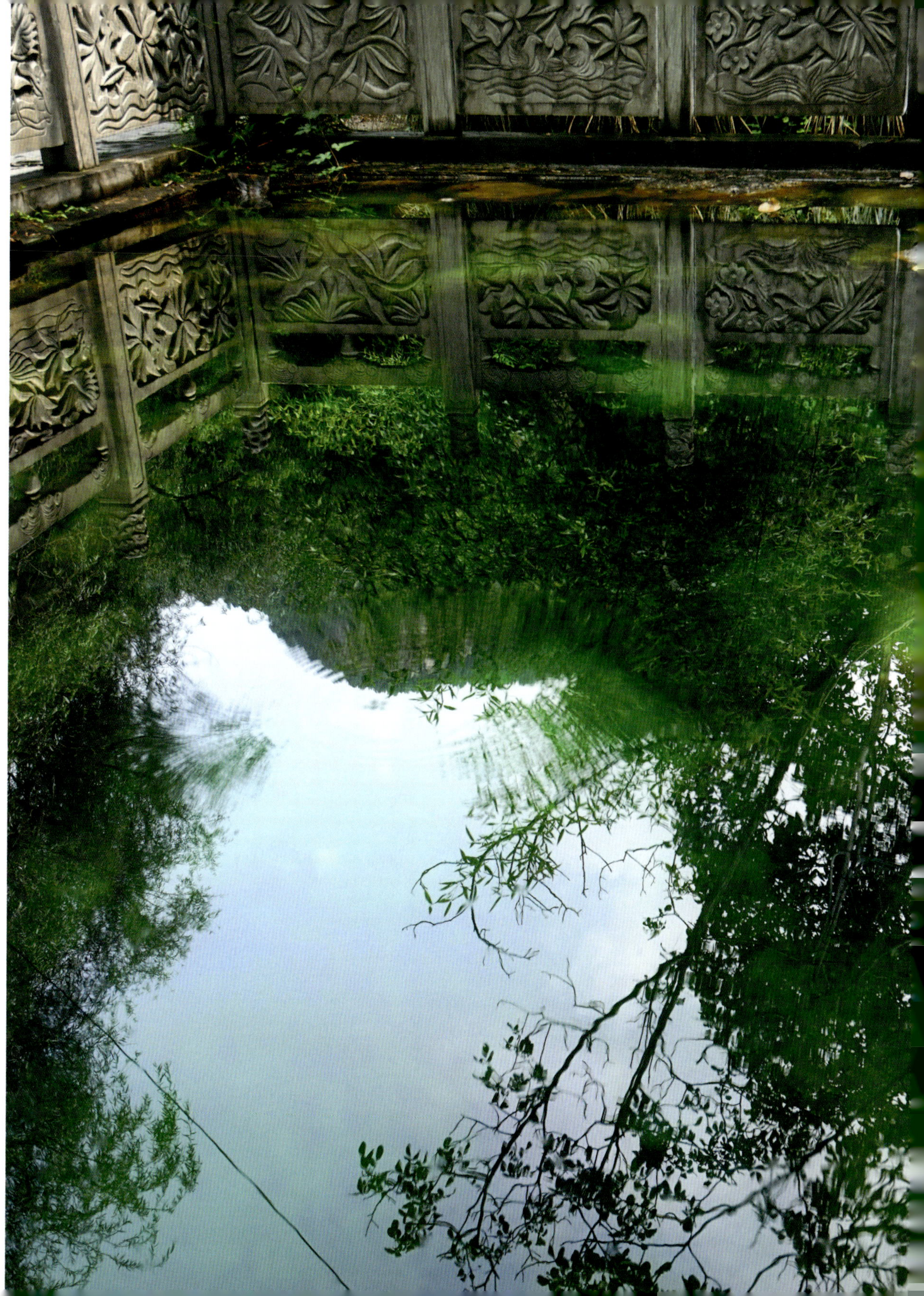

水劲无过济,
脉泉更著名。
不霜清见底,
漱石寂无声。
颗颗如翠珠,
泛泛比镜平。
不能容小艇,
但可濯长缨。

（明）李开先
《游百脉泉一韵五首》其一

百脉泉

百脉泉，因方圆百步内有百泉俱出、合流成湾而得名。古有"西则趵突为魁，东则百脉为冠"的说法。泉水自池底无数脉孔涌出，腾起串串水泡，升浮水面，状如滚动的珍珠，漂荡不息。该泉位于章丘区百脉泉公园明水湖西岸龙泉寺院内。

Baimai Spring

In a circumference of one hundred steps, about a hundred springs spew and converge into an inlet. That's why the spring was named Baimai (a hundred streams). There was an old saying: "Baotu spring is the head of springs in the west, while Baimai is the top of the springs in the east." The water bubbles out from the countless holes at the bottom of the pool and rises up to the surface, just like pearls rolling up and down unceasingly. It is located in the yard of Longquan Temple, which is on the west bank of Mingshui Lake in Baiman Spring Park of Zhangqiu District.

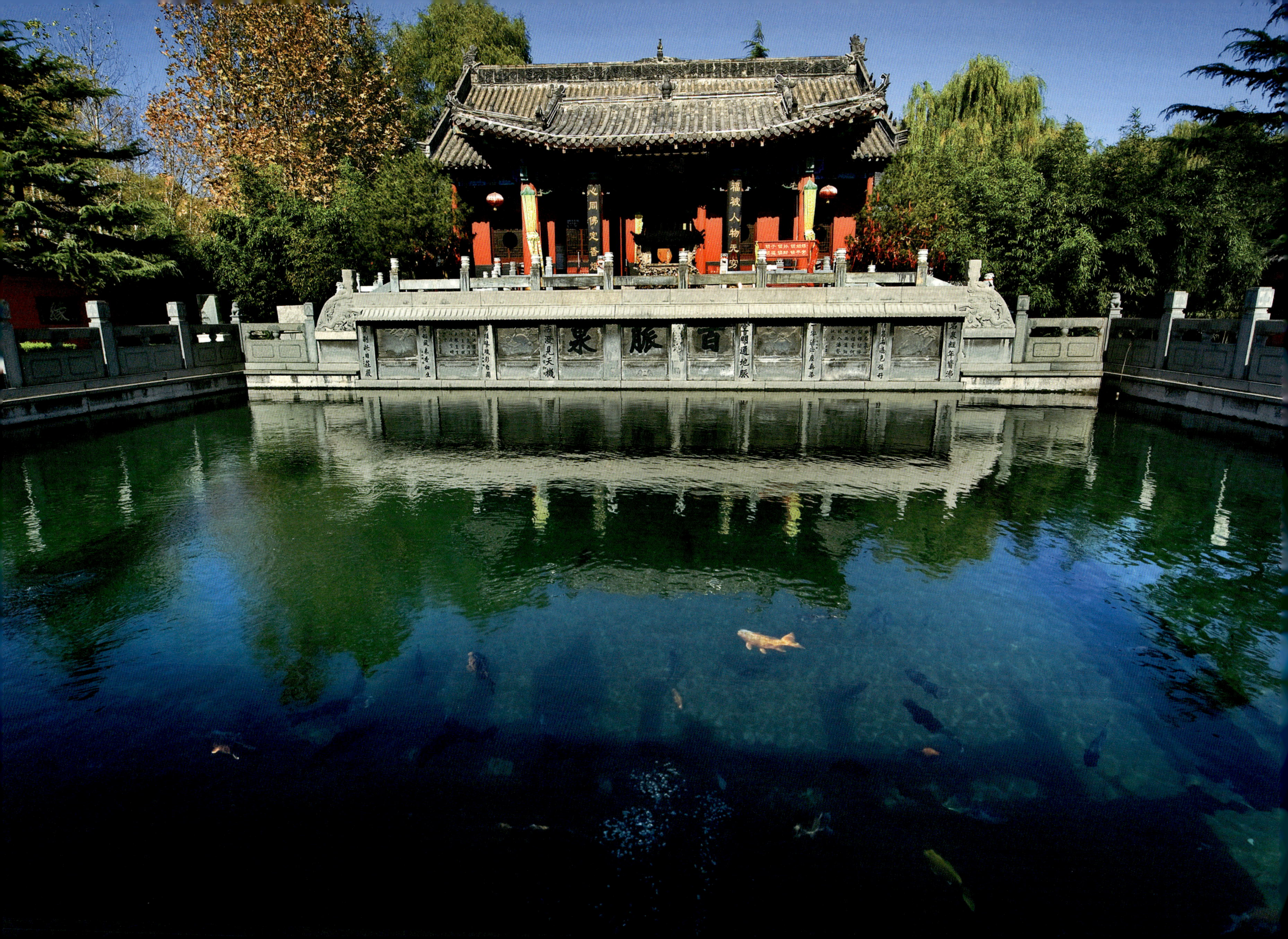
百脉泉

Dongma Pond

The springs within this water area are thickly dotted like stars, so the name "Ma" (dense) was given. Dongma Pond refers to the pond in the east, while Xima Pond refers to the western one. In Dongma Pond, the water spews out and splashes everywhere; waterweeds spread widely; herons play cheerfully. On the banks, the weeping willows stand next to each other; blooming flowers contend in beauty. In size, it is the largest among the famous springs in Jinan. It is to the east of Baimai Spring and in Baiman Spring Park of Zhangqiu District.

东麻湾

因水域内泉若繁星，密密麻麻，故而得名"麻湾"，又因其与西麻湾相别，故称"东麻湾"。东麻湾内，群泉突涌，水花四溅，水草丛生，鸥鹭相戏。岸边垂柳相依，百花争艳。该泉是济南诸泉中水域面积最大的名泉，位于章丘区百脉泉公园内，百脉泉东数十米。

东麻泉众涌成湖，浩量年超一亿余。
远望渚汀荫柳静，近观芦岸片莲徐。
泄玉漱玑泡串串，驱鱼梳草漩窣窣。
拱桥各异连长堤，绣红河源若太虚。
王化学《东麻湾》

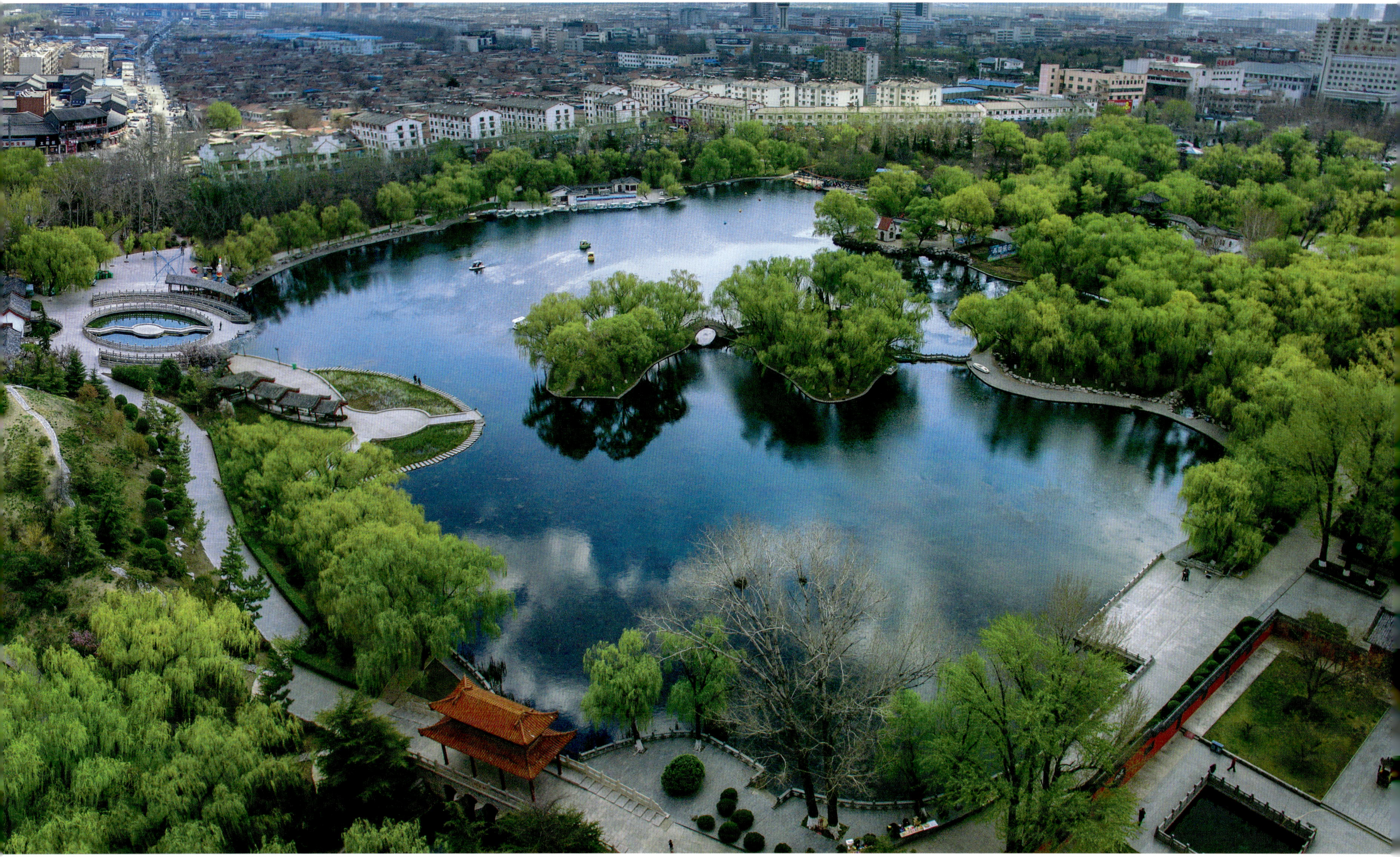

Mo Spring

The color of water is as deep as ink when it spews out, so the spring is named Mo (ink). The gush of water is hemispherical and more than half an inch high. The water looks like boiling and sounds like thundering. The amount of water is constantly large all the year round. The periphery is suffused by steam and fog, which is a charming natural scene. It is in the southwest corner of Longquan Temple in Baiman Spring Park of Zhangqiu District.

墨泉

泉水涌出泉口时，水色深如浓墨，故名"墨泉"。墨泉出露形态为喷涌状，泉水如半球，高出半尺有余，如沸如腾，声若雷鸣，且流量极大，常年无歇。泉池周边，烟波蒸腾，雾霭弥漫，其景观令人叹为观止。该泉位于章丘区百脉泉公园内龙泉寺西南角。

龙泉寺右腾墨泉，天下涌喷观止谈。
乌墨鼓形恍水怪，清汁泻势似龙蟠。
隐雷闷动砚池内，哗雨嘈纷石刻间。
圣释门生通地利，开盘庙址法自然。

王化学《墨泉》

墨泉

穹庐如盖繁星缀,
流光沐楼台。
凭栏处,
梅花漾漾一池水,
丝竹由何来?
疑是天府门未闭,
一曲销魂入梦怀……
恍若宋时月,
依稀李氏宅。
疏朗阁,
竹影婆娑,
少艾清照梳妆处,
槛外清流弄柔苔。
玉枕纱橱,
檀香氤氲,
八哥猫咪,
笑靥浅开;
把盏煮茶,
弄箫鼓瑟,
棋局书画,
垂髫蟋蟀……
千秋往矣,
漱玉今安在?
只留传说,
游人唏嘘,
多情笑我呆!

王化学《墨泉》

梅花泉

泉水自五孔中喷涌而出,恰似一朵盛开的五瓣梅花,故得名"梅花泉"。盛水期,泉水可喷涌高达数尺,鼎沸浪激,云烟蒸腾。旁有李清照故居。该泉位于章丘区百脉泉公园北侧清照园内。

Meihua Spring

The water spews out from 5 drilled holes like a blooming plum flower with 5 petals, so the spring was named Meihua (plum flower). The water can gush inches high, and looks like boiling and steaming. Beside the spring is the former residence of Li Qingzhao. It is in Qingzhao Garden in the north part of Baiman Spring Park of Zhangqiu District.

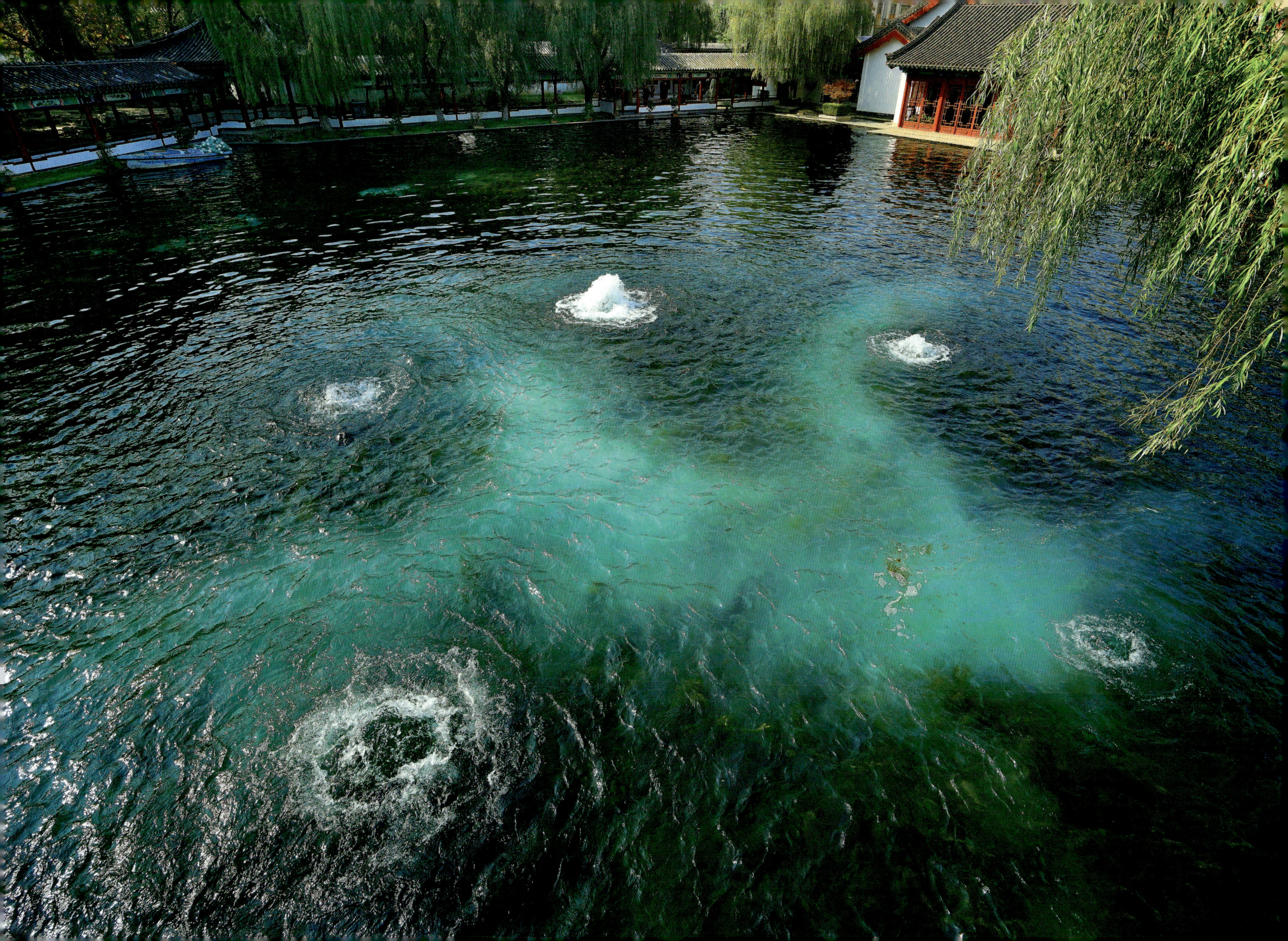

Jingming Spring

The spring is also called Mingjing and Mingshui, for it's close to the Yanmingwang Temple. It is said that anyone who wash eyes with its water can have a clear sight. The gush of water is inches high and splashes around, which is a magnificent scene. The water is extremely clean, and tastes cool and sweet. It is on the north side of Xima Pond, and to the west of Tangzi Bridge in Zhangqiu District.

净明泉

　　净明泉，又称明净泉、明水泉，因原处于眼明王庙旁而得名。传说用此泉泉水洗眼，可以退其昏瞶而令眼清目明。泉水喷涌而出，高达数尺，水花四溅，蔚为壮观；泉水至洁，纤尘不染，清澈见底，味甘如饴。该泉位于章丘区西麻湾北端，塘子桥西侧路北。

清泉一派接银河，
宝鉴同明水不波。
不绕方池闲顾影，
须眉散作百东坡。
（明）晏璧《济南七十二泉诗》

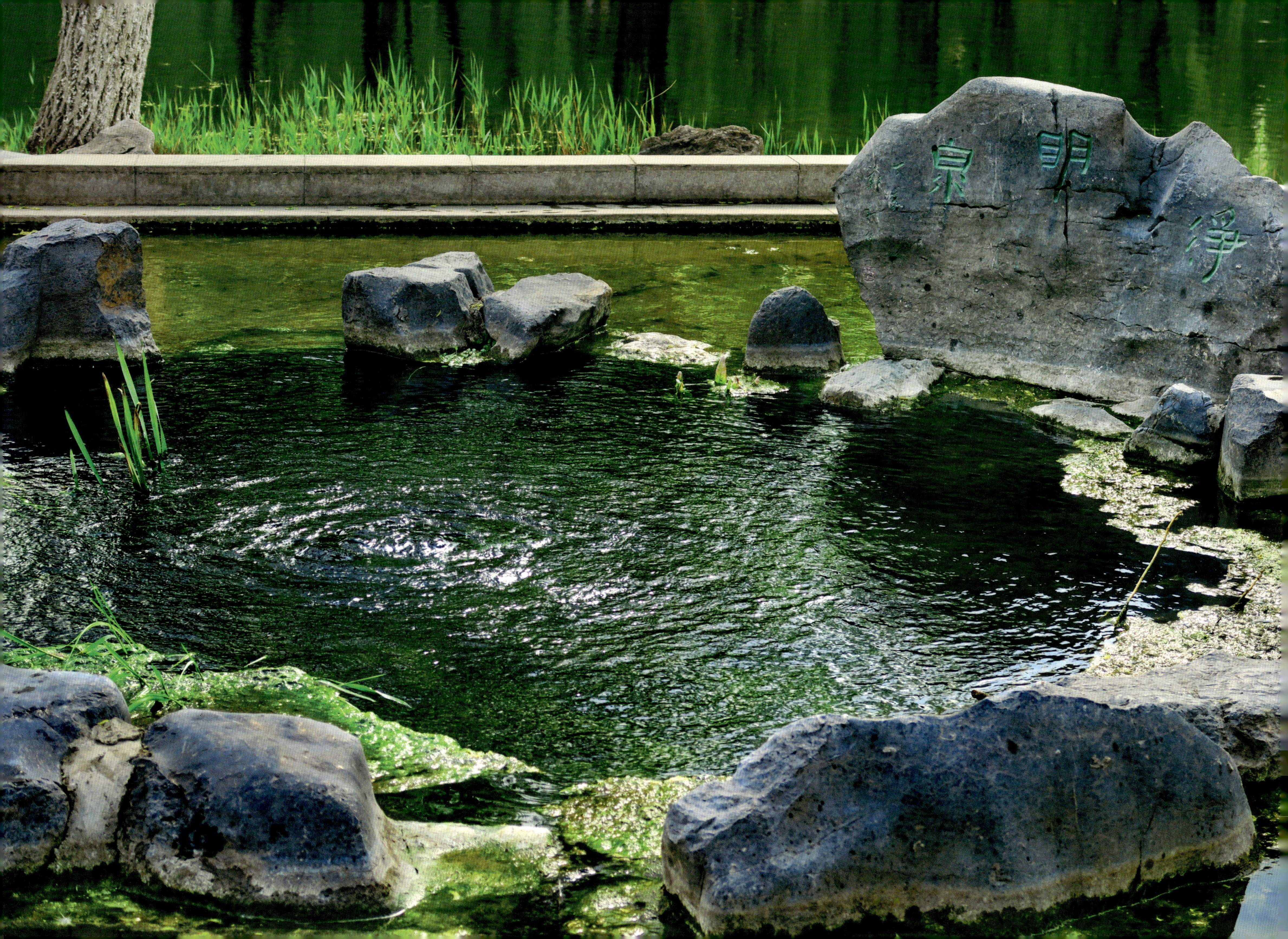
淨明泉

Jiasha Spring

There is a slab of cast iron which looks like a kasaya beside the spring, so the spring is named Jiasha (kasaya). The water spills out from the gaps between the rocks on the hillside and converges into a semicircle pool. Then it overflows into a winding brook and finally pours into the spring pool through the mouth of a stone-carved dragon. It is said that Bodhidharma arrived here from the Western Regions, then faced the wall and mediated for nine years. When the meditation was accomplished, he left his iron kasaya here. It is below the cliff to the east of Zhuanluncang Hall in Lingyan Temple of Changqing District.

袈裟泉

该泉因泉旁立有一块形似袈裟的铸铁而名为"袈裟泉"。水自崖壁石罅流出，汇入一半圆形石潭，溢而为溪，盘桓曲绕，由石雕龙口下泻入池。相传，当年达摩自西域来此面壁九年，道成而去，弃铁袈裟于此。该泉位于长清区灵岩寺"转轮藏"庙堂遗址的东侧路南悬崖下。

我佛慈悲铁作衣,
谁知方便示禅机。
昔年庚岭家风在,
直至如今识者稀。

（宋）释仁钦
《灵岩二十景诗·铁袈裟》

卓
锡
泉

据载，唐代有个叫法定的僧人曾在灵岩山上建造寺庙，但寺庙附近没有水源。于是，他向佛图澄请教，佛图澄走到一处，指着地面说"此地有甘泉"，并用九环锡杖一戳，遂得泉水一眼，故而命名为"卓锡泉"。该泉位于长清区灵岩寺内，千佛殿东侧岩壁下。

Zhuoxi Spring

It is recorded that a monk named Fading built a temple on Mount Lingyan, but he didn't find any water source near the temple. Fading turned to an eminent monk named Fotucheng for help. Fotucheng found a place and pointed to the ground, saying: "There's a spring here." Then he poked the ground with his nine-ring tin cane, and the spring gushed out. Therefore, the spring was named Zhuoxi (poke with tin cane). It is in Lingyan Temple of Changqing District, and below the rocks to the east of Qianfo Hall.

泉临卓锡一亭幽，万壑千岩景毕收。
最喜东南缥纱处，澄公常共朗公游。

（清）爱新觉罗·弘历《卓锡泉》

Qingling Spring

When the water beats the rocks, it produces a "ling" sound, which is like the sound of playing qin and se (two traditional Chinese musical instruments). Therefore, the spring is named Qingling. The spring is beneath the Zhixian Pavilion on Mount Wufeng of Changqing District, and on the east side of Dongzhen Temple. Dongzhen Temple is one of the largest Taoist temples in the north of Yangtze River. Qingling Spring, as the best spring in the temple, has "three wonders": the musical sound of spring water, a thousand-year-old monoecious ginkgo, and making tea without leaving scale.

清泠泉

清泠泉，因泉水激石，泠泠作响，犹如有人抚弄琴瑟而得名。该泉位于济南市长清区五峰山志仙亭下，洞真观玉皇殿东侧。洞真观是江北较大的道教圣地，此泉也被誉为观内"第一名泉"。清泠泉有三绝：一曰泉水淙淙，叮咚悦耳；二曰雌雄银杏，同株千载；三曰烹茶无垢，尘襟涤尽。

入尘无意出尘难，
半在山林半在官。
两袖清风登峻岭，
冰心一片对甘澜。

（清）王弘任《无题》

清冷泉

檀抱泉

因泉穴上方岩壁上有一株千年青檀俯抱此泉，故名"檀抱泉"。青檀因泉水滋润长势旺盛，枝繁叶茂；泉受青檀庇护，长年喷涌，四季不歇。该泉位于长清区万德镇明孔山下第四峪村。

Tanbao Spring

The spring was embraced by a thousand-year-old Pteroceltis tree growing on the rock above, so it was named Tanbao (embraced by a Pteroceltis tree). The tree is nourished by the spring water, so it is strong and leafy; the spring is protected by the tree, so it spews all the year round. It is below Mingkong Mountain in Wande Town of Changqing District.

树密鸟啼青嶂晓，
塔高钟和白云深。
闲看贝叶通禅意，
静听灵泉不醉心。
（明）戴燿《无题》节选

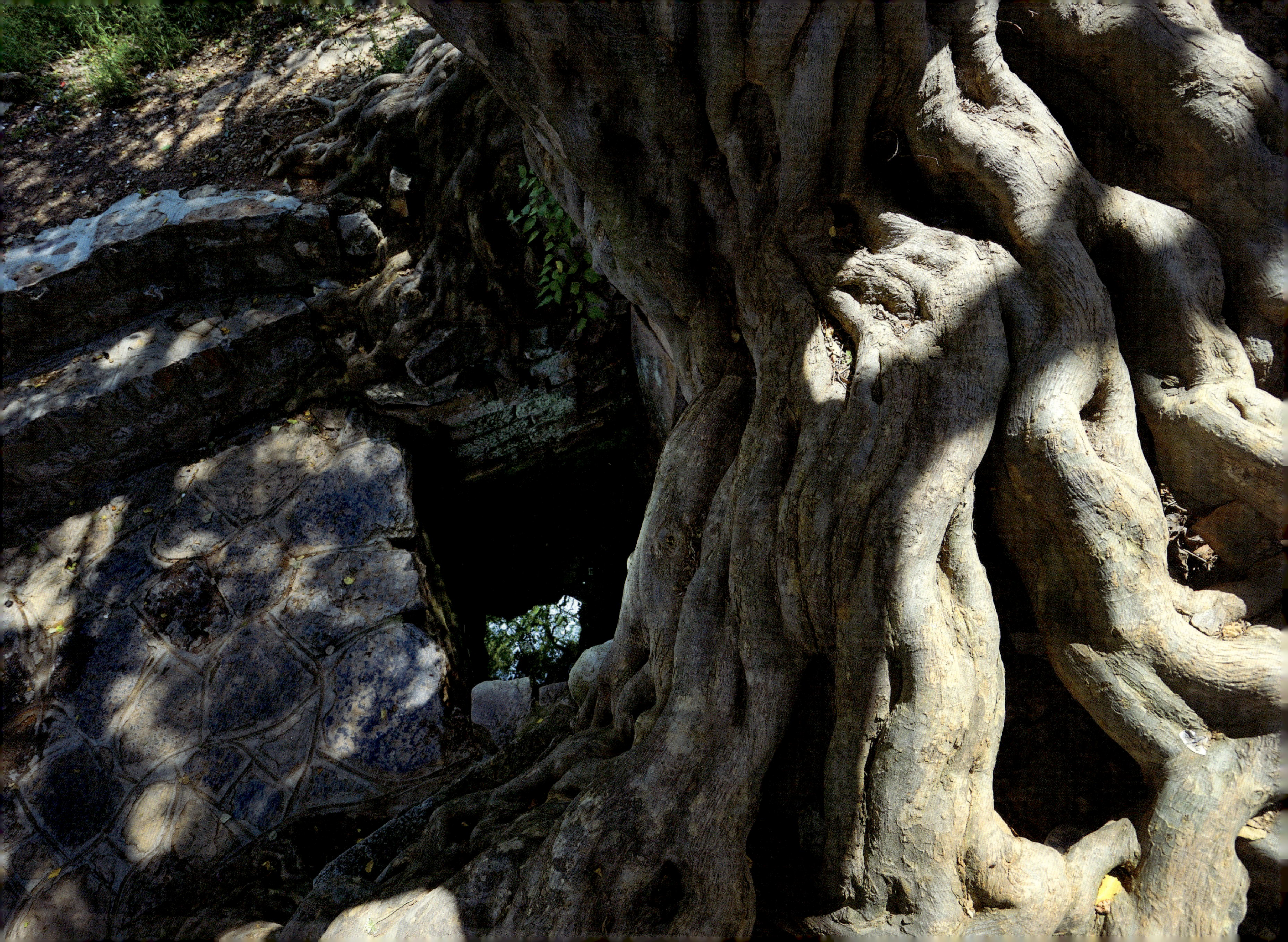

晓露泉

相传泉水系晨露凝聚而成，故名"晓露泉"。该泉从岩洞石隙中喷涌而出，流经暗渠，从一白玉雕刻的龙口泻进池中。泉洞上方有一棵千年古柏，树北有一株虬曲的青藤攀缘其上，两树同生，古奇两妙，遂成一景。该泉位于长清区张夏镇积米峪村北一石洞中。

> 洞顶参天古柏，穴内森凉泉井。山被青茏葱翠，水由晓露凝成。格局成于洪武，外池仿而新兴。天时地利人和，列属灵岩八景。
>
> 王化学《晓露泉》

Xiaolu Spring

It is said that the spring is converged by morning dews, so it is named Xiaolu (morning dew). The water spills out from the gaps between the cave rocks, flows in culverts, and finally pours into the spring pool through the mouth of a jade-carved dragon. There is a thousand-year-old cypress growing above the spring cave, with twisted green ivy winding upon its bole. Their harmonious coexistence composes an interesting picture. It is in a cave at the north end of Jimiyu Village in Zhangxia Town of Changqing District.

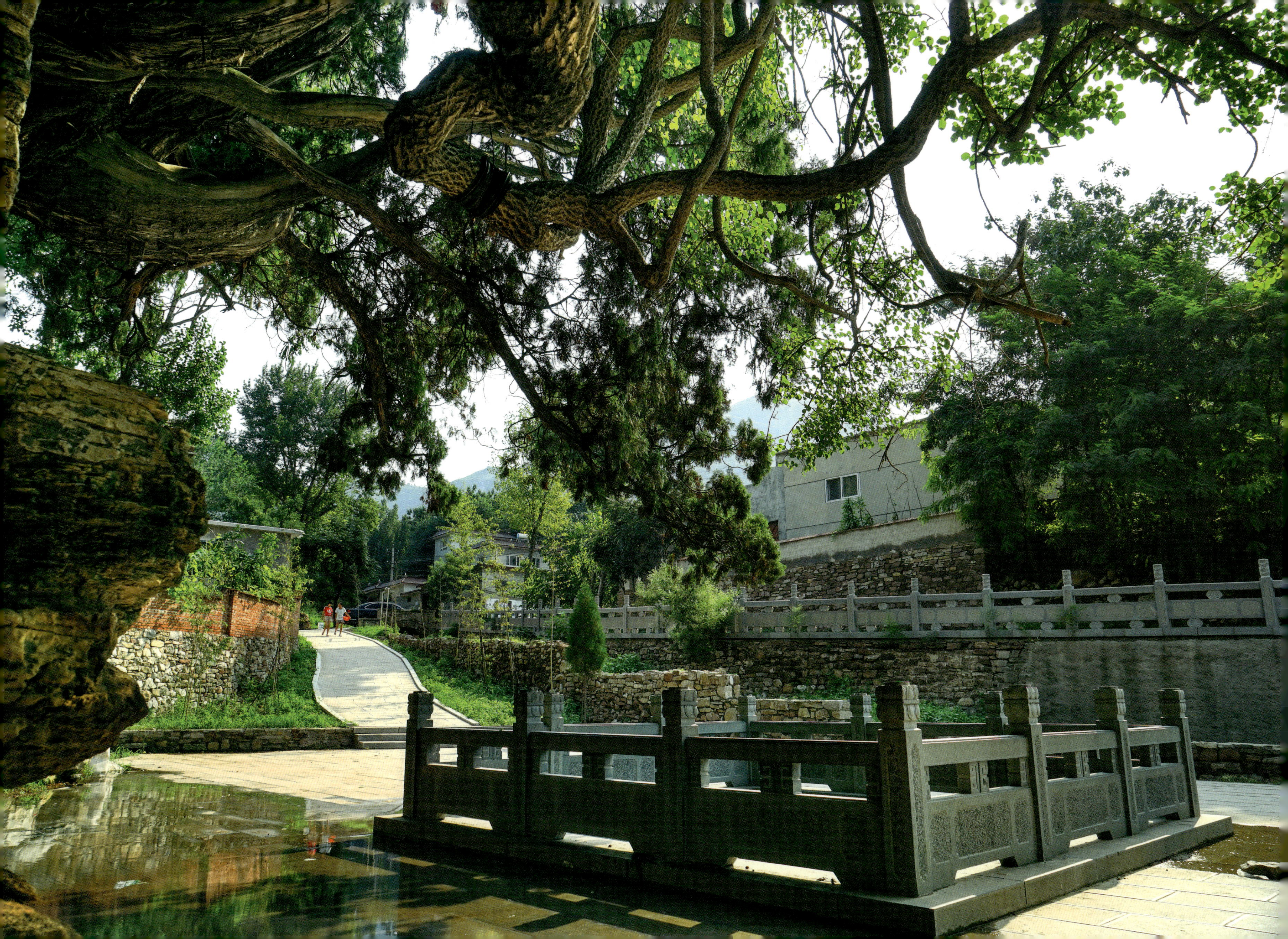

洪范池

"洪范"一词出自《尚书·洪范》篇，取"洪水就范"之意。金代，当地百姓因祈求风调雨顺、洪水不再泛滥，在泉北修建龙祠一座，故洪范池又称为"龙池"，距今已有八九百年历史。游人掷硬币于池中，上涌泉水使硬币漂动而不沉，日照其上，金光闪闪。该泉位于平阴县洪范池公园内。

方池十丈水之浮，
洪范锡名称到今。
戏掷一钱清澈底，
随波荡漾似浮金。

（明）何海晏《洪范浮金》

Hongfan Pond

Hongfan, meaning "the flood is tamed", is derived from *Shangshu*. In the Jin Dynasty, in order to pray for good weather, local people built a Long (dragon) Temple on the north side of the spring. Therefore, the spring is also called Long Spring, and it has a history of eight or nine hundred years. The coins, thrown into the pool by visitors, drift with water upwards and do not sink easily. When sunlight sprinkles on the coins, you'll see a magic scene of floating gold. It is located in Hongfan Pond Park of Pingyin County.

池龍

书院泉

此泉因水往东流，古称"东流泉"，泉名首见于1500多年前的北魏《水经注》。明朝嘉靖年间，老臣刘隅告老返乡，在泉畔构建精舍，并主持东流书院，并将泉名改为"书院泉"。该泉泓澄莹澈，毛发可鉴，环境清雅，景色迷人。该泉位于平阴县洪范池镇书院村东首天池山脚下。

Shuyuan Spring

In the past, the spring was called Dongliu (flow eastward) for its flowing direction. The name first appeared in *Shuijing Zhu* which was written more than 1500 years ago. In the Ming Dynasty, an official named Liu Yu retired on account of age, and built a gorgeous building beside the spring. He chaired Dongliu Academy, and renamed the spring Shuyuan (academy). The water is extremely clean and the ambient scenery is elegant and charming. It is below the Tianchi Mountain at the east end of Shuyuan Village in Hongfanchi Town of Pingyin County.

风雨鸣丹谷，林亭倚翠岑。
一樽今日酒，千里故人心。
树勤三秋色，泉飞万壑音。
夜凉横吹起，欲听水龙吟。

（明）于慎行《游书院泉》

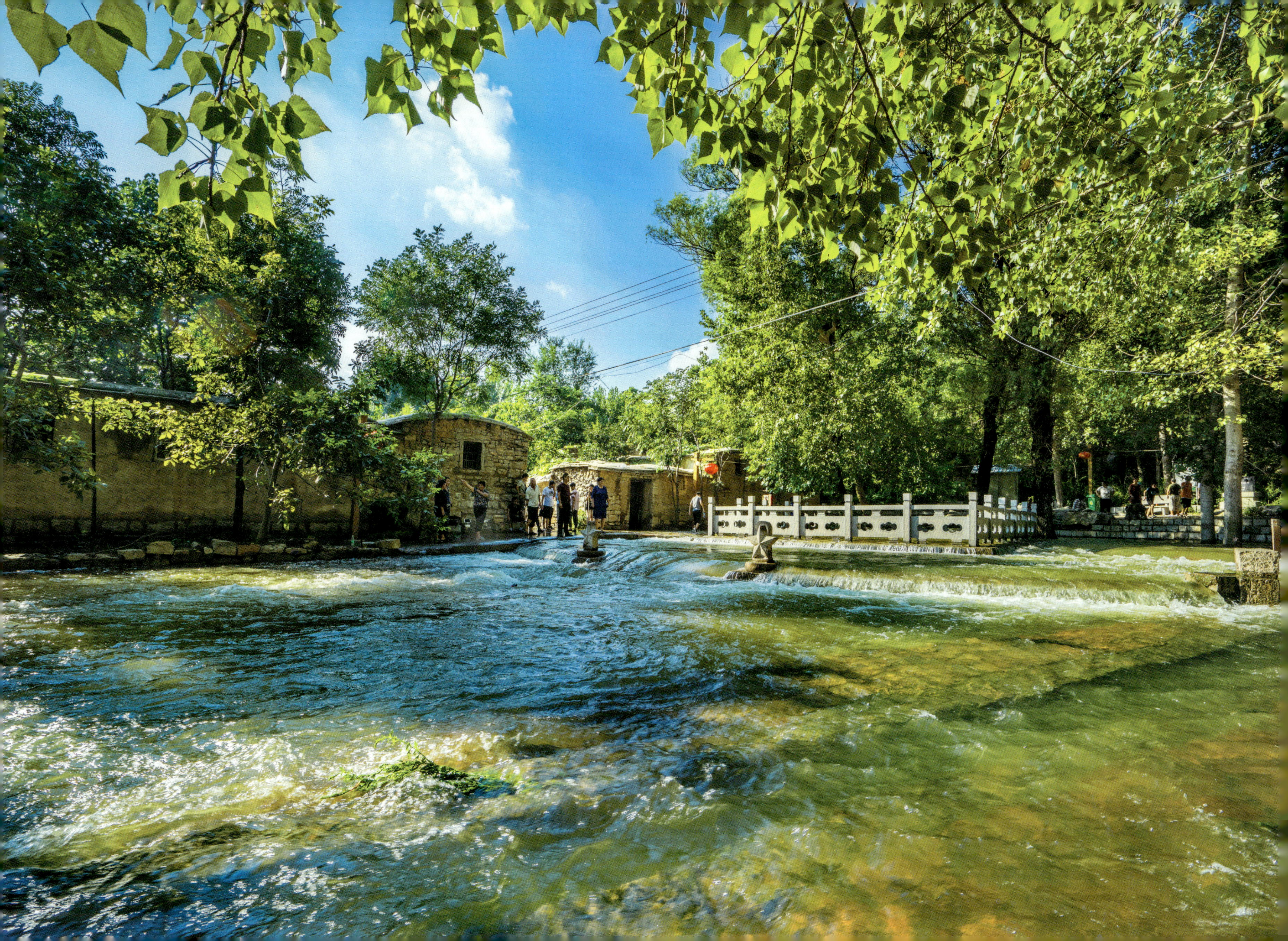

冲崖上出有飞泉,
倒泻争如瀑布悬。
抵石触岩喷似雪,
胜他玉碎又珠圆。

佚名 见康熙《东阿县志》

Hu Spring

The spring was named Hu mainly for its location. In history, the spring was close to the capital of the state of Hu. Furthermore, it is located in the Mount Hu Col on the north slop of Mount Yuncui in Pingyin County. The spring spews out from a cave, and is blocked by the rocks at the mouth of the cave, with foams splashing around like flying snow. The water pours down in a waterfall and beats the cliff and rocks, producing sounds that can be heard miles away. It is about 2 kilometers southward from the government of Hongfanchi Town of Pingyin District, and in a col below the north side of Yuncui Mountain.

扈
泉

因泉水北临古扈国都城，又处平阴云翠山北麓扈山坳，故名"扈泉"。扈泉从山洞中喷涌而出，遇其洞口巨石塞堵，珠沫四溅，状如飞雪，呈瀑布状奔泻而下，触岩抵石，声传数里。该泉位于平阴县洪范池镇政府南约2公里，云翠山北麓的扈山山坳里。

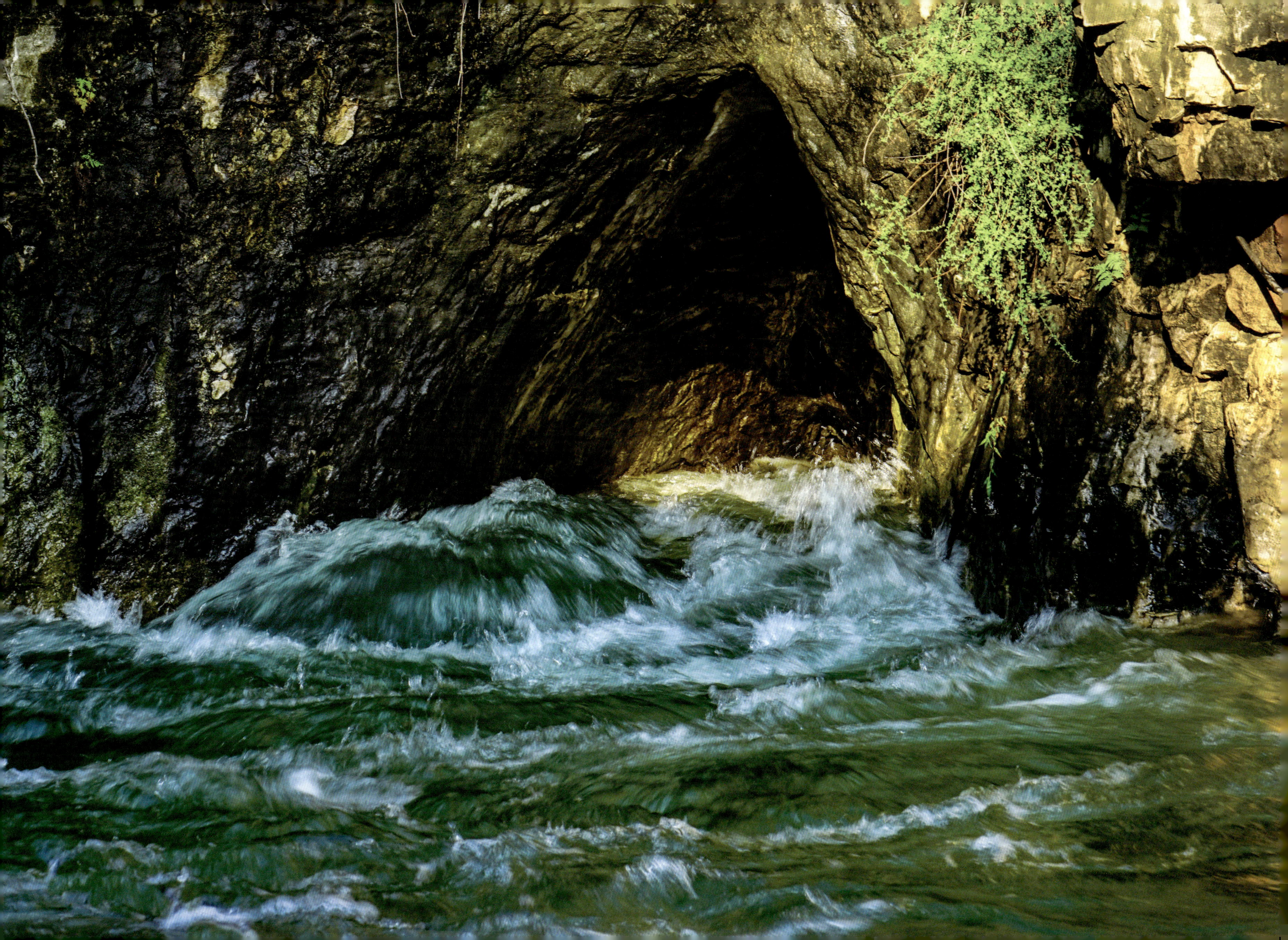

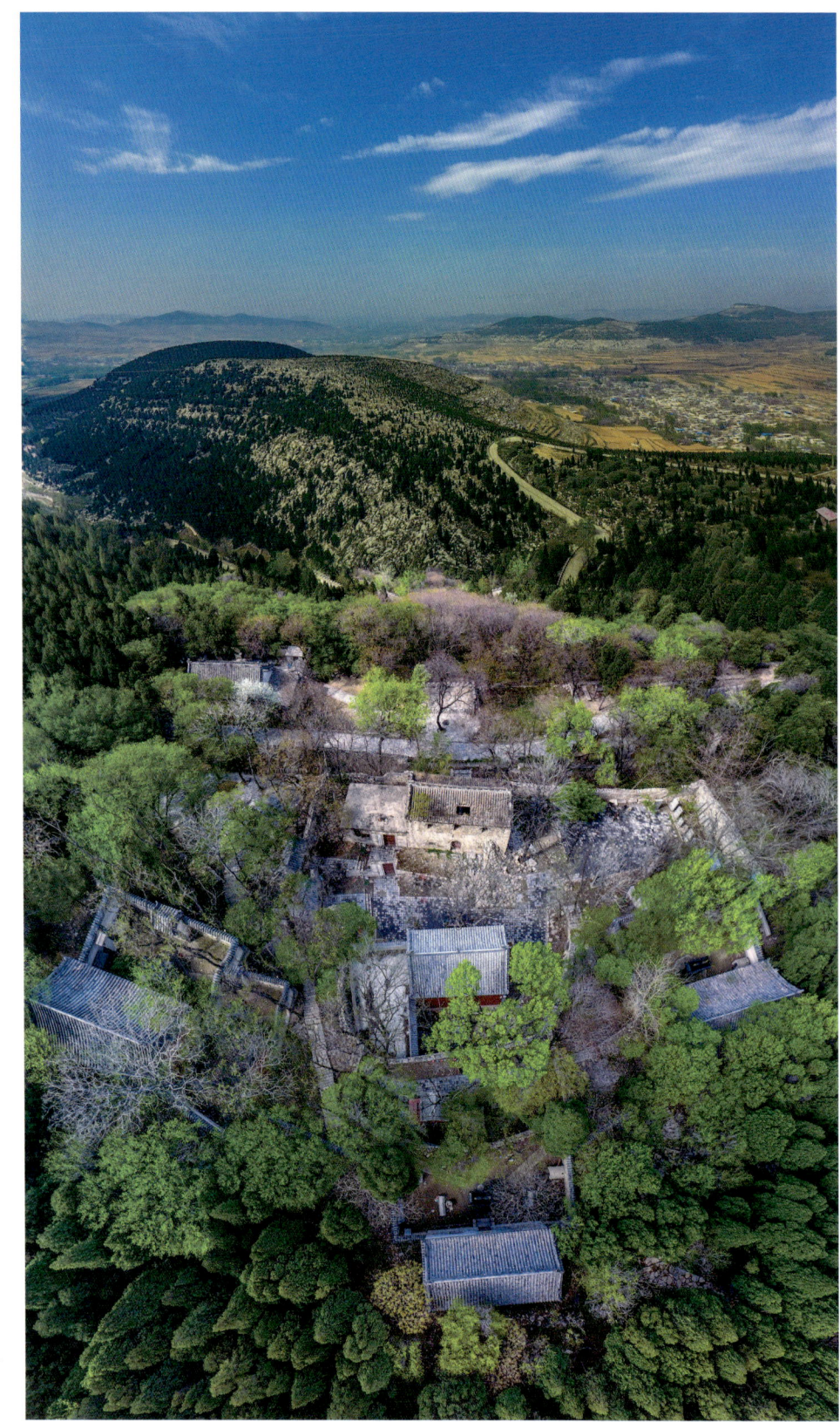

日月泉

泉水自洞底渗出，形成一泓清池，池上覆盖一块石板，石板刻有双孔，一孔圆似太阳，一孔半圆如月。朝暮之时，阳光斜射入洞，透过两孔，隐约可见水面日月之影，犹如日月争辉，故得名"日月泉"。该泉位于平阴县洪范池镇南部的云翠山南天观回阳洞内。

Riyue Spring

The water spills from the bottom of the cave, forms a pool. The pool is covered by a slate with two holes. The circular hole is in the shape of the sun, and the semi-circular one is the shape of the moon. The sunlight goes through the holes, forming the reflections of the sun and the moon. Therefore, the spring on Mount Yuncui was named Riyue (the sun and the moon). It is in Huiyang Cave of Nantian Temple on Yuncui Mountain in the south of Hongfanchi Town of Pingyin District.

日和月，
阿波罗与狄安娜，
同胞孪生、交相辉映。
美丽神话——
形貌相当、个性殊别：
一团烈火，
情至痴处成灰烬；
一弯冷影，
冰清玉洁贵寂寞……

王化学《日月泉》

后记

我是土生土长、地地道道的济南人,从小就喜水、爱泉。年轻时第一次端起相机,拍的就是趵突泉、大明湖。在此后的漫长岁月里,无论是军旅生涯,还是到地方工作,我对家乡的泉水始终有一种难以割舍的情怀。

近年来,济南市委市政府高度重视对泉水的保护和利用,把弘扬泉水文化、建设现代泉城作为重要举措,加快推进济南的全面建设。我在长期的摄影实践中深深感到,用影像真实地记录当下泉水的风貌,艺术地再现泉水的无穷魅力,是一件十分有意义的事情,也是摄影人尤其是济南摄影人义不容辞的历史担当。这件事做好了,不仅能为社会留存一份当今济南泉水的系统资料,也能给百姓提供一份赏泉、品泉、爱泉的精神食粮。

在我的眼里,泉水是有生命、有灵性的。为了拍出对泉水的理解和感悟,把泉水的特色、韵味淋漓尽致地体现出来,我在拍摄过程中注意了这样几点:

一是以拍好名泉为重点。济南泉水众多,分布广泛,仅全市辖区内泉水就有 800 余处。我把主要精力和重点放在对七十二名泉的拍摄上,对每个名泉反复思考揣摩,选择不同季节、不同时段进行拍摄,有些名泉先后拍过数次乃至数十次。

二是全方位多角度立体拍摄。我学习了无人机航拍和水下摄影技术,从空中、地面、水下,多视角地记录反映泉水的面貌。试图通过这些手段,使图像更具视觉冲击力,让人们对泉水有全新的感受。

三是坚持纪实性与艺术性的统一。拍摄泉水必须客观真实,但也要讲究艺术性。为了把两者较好地统一起来,我选择了在不同季节、不同天气条件下,采取多种方式进行拍摄,以增强泉水摄影作品的美感和艺术感染力。

这本画册是从我拍摄的 30000 余幅泉水照片中精选出来的。这是我多年拍泉的一个小结,也是向家乡人民的一次汇报。这件事自始至终得到中共济南市委宣传部、济南市人民政府新闻办公室的指导和支持;惠苅林、周玉山、孙志荣、于峰、张泉刚、宋丽英、赵继福等山东省艺术摄影学会及有关方面的同志抽出宝贵时间陪同我拍摄,帮助整理资料,进行后期制作;著名书法家刘锡山撰写书名。在此谨向大家表示衷心感谢!

李华文

2019 年 5 月

Postscript

As a native of Jinan, I have loved water and springs since childhood. The first time I took up my camera when I was young, the pictures I took were Baotu Spring and Daming Lake. Since then, whenever I was in the army or during my civilian life, I have always adored the springs of my hometown.

In recent years, the city of Jinan has given special attention to the preservation of springs in order to promote the culture of springs, build a modern city, and speed up the comprehensive development of Jinan. I believe that using photography to capture the springs and artistically represent the beauty of the springs is a very meaningful task and a responsibility of a Jinan photographer. If done well, it would be a good documentation of the springs systems in Jinan, it would also be a gift to the citizens of Jinan.

In my eyes, springs are alive. The hardest part of photographing springs is how to understand the springs and how to vividly depict the uniqueness of each springs. To achieve these goals, I paid attention to the following points:

My first focus is to photograph all the renowned springs. There are around 800 springs in and around Jinan. I focused on the 72 most well-known springs. I studied each spring and chose to photograph each one during different seasons and different times of the day, in some cases tens of times for each spring, in order to capture the true beauty of each.

My second focus is to photograph from all-round and multiple angles. I used aerial and underwater techniques in addition to traditional techniques to photograph every angle of the springs. This way, the springs can be viewed from strikingly new perspectives.

My third focus is to integrate realism and artistry. To photograph springs, it must be objective and realistic. In order to integrate these two goals, I photographed the same springs at night and during the day, during different seasons and different weather conditions, and used human models during shooting in order to increase the artistic appeal of the photographs.

I have chosen these pictures out of 30,000 pictures of the springs to include in this album. It is a brief summary of my work over the years and a small gift to the people of my hometown. The Publicity Department of the Government of Jinan and the News Office of the Government of Jinan have rendered strong support for this initiative since the very beginning. Several friends from the Shandong Artistic Photography Association: Mr. Shulin Hui, Mr. Yushan Zhou, Mr. Zhirong Sun, Mr. Feng Yu, Mr. Quangang Zhang, Ms. Liying Song, and Mr. Jifu Zhao spent their valuable time to accompany me to shoot around the city, organize materials, and process photos. Renowned calligrapher Mr. Xishan Liu calligraphed the title of the album. I sincerely appreciate all those who have helped with the editing and production of the album.

Huawen Li
2019.5

《一城泉水》编委会

主　任
杨　峰

顾　问
侯贺良

副主任
孙常建　周　明　赵　民　王亮朝

编　委
李华文　孙清华　王化学　张宝宗　罗云平　牛　钧

主　编
赵　民　王亮朝

编　辑
石舒波　荣　荣　苏　里　李德辰

摄　影
李华文

撰　文（除署名外）
张继平

翻　译
王　潇　李一潭　张恩煜

校　译
李钰欣

整体设计
牛　钧